GR

Coffee around the World

Featuring.....

- Over 250 coffee brands
- In 70 countries
- Across 6 continents

Web Guides International LLC | New York

Grahame's Guides™ is an imprint of
Web Guides International LLC.

This book or parts thereof may not be reproduced in any form, stored in any retrieval system, or transmitted in any form by any means—electronic, mechanical, photocopy, recording, or otherwise—without prior written permission of the publisher, except as provided by United States of America copyright law.

While we have sought to provide accurate, up-to-date information, it is subject to change and error. Please check directly with companies listed as to food allergies or other issues that may concern you.

Copyright © 2021
Web Guides International LLC
All Rights Reserved.

Printed in the United States of America

ISBN-13: 978-1-7327005-3-6

Web Guides International LLC
57 West 57th Street, 4th floor
New York, NY 10019
info@grahamesguides.com
www.GrahamesCoffeeGuide.com

www.grahamescoffeeguide.com

CONTENTS

Page 4	Introduction
Page 5	Coffee History, Facts & Numbers
Page 15	European Coffee
Page 43	U.S. and Canadian Coffee
Page 74	Latin American Coffee
Page 93	Asia/Mideast/African Coffee
Page 110	Coffee Festivals
Page 114	Coffee Glossary
Page 116	Coffee, Fair Trade and Sustainability
Page 117	Coffee in 95 Languages
Page 119	Alphabetical Index

INTRODUCTION

Wherever we live in the world, there is one thing nearly every person wakes up to: coffee.

It is how we start our day. For many coffee lovers, it is also what gets us through the day – and for much of coffee's history, most people were happy with the coffee they had. Or they simply didn't know better.

However, the past decade has seen a veritable explosion in the quality – and variety – of the coffee available to consumers. Moreover, coffee drinkers have become infinitely more knowledgeable and discriminating about the coffee they purchase.

The source of the bean and how it is processed to bring out the most exquisite flavors is a matter of intense debate. Is light or dark roast better? Colombian or Vietnamese beans? The list goes on.

Here in this handy guidebook we honor them all – and give to the reader, we hope, a convenient way to begin their own personal exploration of what in the grand spectrum of coffees suits their *own* individual gustatory sensibility.

Indeed, to borrow an expression, it is not only time to smell the coffee. It is a great time to smell many different coffees!

www.grahamescoffeeguide.com

COFFEE:
A BRIEF HISTORY

800 AD	**Ethiopian** herdsman Kaldi notices his goats are feeling more energetic after chewing certain red berries. He shares the news with a nearby monastery, which also begins partaking. Elsewhere in Ethiopia, the Galla tribe wraps the red berries in animal fat, producing the very first "power bar."
1000	**Yemeni** traders returning from Ethiopia begin cultivating the coffee plant and mix its berries with boiling water to create "qahwa" which means "that which prevents sleep."
1450s	Coffee is introduced to the **Turkish** metropolis of Constantinople where locals mix it with such spices as clove, cardamom, and cinnamon.
1511	In **Mecca**, the governor forbids coffee, worried that more energetic discussions could lead to challenging his rule. However, his boss in Cairo overrules him, has him executed – yikes! – and declares coffee sacred.
1600s	Coffee reaches **Venice**. Some locals declare it the devil's drink. But Pope Clement VIII tries and likes coffee so much that he gives it his blessing!

1650s	Europe sees rapid growth of coffeehouses. In just London alone, there are about 300 of them. Coffee replaces beer as the way to start your day.
1774	American colonials stage the famous Boston Tea Party revolt against heavy British taxes. Result: coffee replaces tea as the most popular local drink.
1822	Louis Bernard Bahbaut invents a prototype espresso machine, but it is fellow Frenchman Edward Santais who later commercializes his own version, wowing visitors at the Paris Exposition of 1855.
1865	New Zealand's David Strang stakes claim to the world's first commercially available instant coffee with his patented powder made with boiling water.
1903	Sanka, the first decaffeinated coffee, is created after German merchant Ludwig Roselius accidentally soaks his coffee beans in seawater.
1920	U.S. Coffee sales boom after the government's prohibition against alcohol goes into effect.
1938	Nestle invents freeze-dried coffee as a solution to Brazil's surplus of coffee beans.
1971	Starbucks, today the world's largest coffee chain, opens its first store in Seattle.

COFFEE FACTS & NUMBERS

3	The average number of cups of coffee that Americans drink daily.
$3.28	The average price of a cup of coffee in the United States.
35%	The percent of coffee drinkers who consume their coffee black.
50	The number of countries around the world which grow coffee.
65%	The percent of Americans who drink coffee with their breakfast.
70	The approximate number of coffee beans it takes to make a cup of coffee.
$5.2 billion	The dollar amount of annual coffee retail sales in the United States.
400 billion	Number of cups of coffee served worldwide each year, making coffee the globe's most favored beverage.
37,274	The total number of coffee shops in the U.S.

www.grahamescoffeeguide.com

Top Coffee PRODUCERS	Brazil, Vietnam, Colombia, Hondurus, India, Indoneisa.

Top Coffee CONSUMERS (per capita per year)	Finland (12kg), Norway (9.9kg), Iceland (9.0kg), Denmark (8.7kg), Netherlands (8,4kg), Sweden (8.2kg), Switzerland (7.9kg), Belgium (6.8kg).

Coffea	This is the scientific name for the coffee plant which is part of the Rubiaceae family.

"Woman Taking Coffee" by Louis Marin Bonnet (1774)

www.grahamescoffeeguide.com

Did you know....

- Coffee is the second-largest internationally traded legal commodity, trailing only oil.

- Brazil is the leading grower of coffee beans, producing one-third of the world total.

- Coffee happens to be the biggest source of antioxidants in the Western diet - outranking both fruits and vegetables combined.

- A regular cup of coffee actually has more caffeine than an espresso – 120 milligrams vs. 80 milligrams

- Coffee "beans" are in fact the seeds of coffee cherries, a fruit.

- Johann Sebastian Bach wrote a song about coffee, known as "The Coffee Cantata."

BOSTON EXCHANGE COFFEE HOUSE, BUILT 1808...BURNT 1818.

www.grahamescoffeeguide.com

THE GLOBAL COFFEE ROASTERS

While much of this guide features smaller, local coffee roasters, below we recognize some of the global giants who daily keep millions of coffee drinkers happy the world over:

Costa Coffee	This UK coffee chain has come a long way since brothers Bruno and Sergio Costa founded it in 1971 -- operating now in some 32 countries. In 2019, it was purchased by the Coca Cola Co. www.costacoffee.com
Dunkin'	With 12,000 outlets in 38 countries, Dunkin' is one of the most popular coffees on Earth. Yet it all started with a single Boston-area shop in 1948 – the idea of businessman William Rosenberg. www.dunkindonuts.com
Folgers	Founded in San Francisco in 1850, Folgers is one of the oldest coffee brands in the U.S. and at times it has been the #1 coffee brand in America. www.folgerscoffee.com
Illy	In 1930, Francesco Illy had an idea for a new coffee business. Today his Italian roasting company is present in some 140 countries! It remains in the family, led by the third generation. www.illy.com

JAB Holding	You may have never heard of JAB Holding, but you surely know the German conglomerate's coffee brands: Caribou, Gevalia, Green Mountain, Hill Bros., Kauai, Peet's, Stumptown, and Tully's, among others. www.jabholco.com
Lavazza	When Luigi Lavazza launched this brand from his small grocery store in Turin, Italy, in 1895, who imagined it would grow so far and wide? Today, Lavazza is sipped and enjoyed in over 90 countries. www.lavazza.com
Massimo Zanetti	While Italians know this company for its Segafredo Zanetti brand, others may know its other famous lines, such as Chock Full o' Nuts, Segafredo, Chase & Sanborn, and others. www.mzb-group.com
Maxwell House	Maxwell House has been around over 100 years and is one of the best-loved coffee brands in American homes. They can thank Joel Owsley Cheek, a small grocer in Nashville who introduced it. www.myfoodandfamily.com/brands/maxwell-house
McCafe	In 1993, Australian licensee Anne Brown came up with the idea of introducing a coffee house chain for McDonald's. Well, it worked! Today there are some 15,000 of them around the world. www.mccdonalds.com

Nescafe	In 1930, Brazil had a lot of surplus coffee beans, so Switzerland's Nestle came up with it's now-famous instant coffee – Nescafe – which today can be found almost anywhere you go. www.nescafe.com
Starbucks	With over 25,000 stores in some 70 countries, Starbucks is hands-down the largest coffee chain in the world. And to think that it all started in 1971 in Seattle with just a single store! www.starbucks.com
Tim Horton's	Started by a famous hockey player in 1964, this popular Canadian chain has grown to have a presence today in some 14 countries. In 2014, the chain was purchased by Burger King. www.timhortons.com

Men Dancing in a Coffee House (London, 1793)

www.grahamescoffeeguide.com

THE PRICIEST COFFEES

Among specialty coffees, these are perhaps the most extraordinary – in taste, method, and especially price. Each is truly one of a kind!

Black Ivory	At $1,000/lb., Thailand's Black Ivory is made most unusually: by feeding coffee beans to elephants and then collecting their, uh, waste. What can we say? www.blackivorycoffee.com
Hacienda La Esmerelda	Grown in Panama's Boquete highlands, this award-winning coffee goes for up to $600/lb. Reason: the beans come from rare Geisha varietals often in short supply. www.haciendaesmereldacom
Ospina Grand Cru	Ospina is one of Colombia's oldest coffee plantations. This most prized of their products grows in volcanic ash at some 7,500 ft. above sea level. www.ospinacoffee.com
Finca el Injerto	Grown by Guatemala's Aguirre family, now in its fourth generation, this highly coveted coffee is known for its fruity and floral flavors. www.fincaelinjerto.com
St. Helena Coffee	It wasn't all bad for Napoleon after his exile to this Atlantic island. Turns out they have great coffee, made from rare, green-tipped bourbon seeds. www.st-helena-coffee.com

Abbreviation Key

Coffee roasters with the following notations offer at least *some* products of this kind, according to our research. However, to be 100% certain, please be sure to contact them directly for confirmation.

FT	Fair Trade
🍃	Organic
S	Single Origin

Ⓛ	Light Roast
Ⓜ	Medium Roast
Ⓓ	Dark Roast

☕	Capuccino
☕	Espresso
ⓓ	Decaffeinated
C	Cold Brew

Please note: Brief quotations in the listings are from the coffee roasters' websites and are intended to help provide insight into their approach and processes.

EUROPE

AUSTRIA

What elicits caffeine thoughts more than a Viennese café? It is said that coffee got its start here after the Turks ended their siege of the city in 1683, leaving behind bags of coffee beans. With those in hand, an enterprising officer by the name of Georg Franz Kolschitzky opened the nation's first coffee house.

CoffeePirates
Est.2012 by Evelyn Priesch and Werner Savernik
Spitalgasse 17
1090 Vienna
Tel: +43 660 342 1411
www.coffeepirates.at

"Our goal is to source, roast and craft the finest coffees from outstanding coffee farms around the world. We travel to origin countries at least twice a year with the aim of creating transparency and traceability."

Jonas Reindl
Est. 2014 by Philip Feyer
Westbahnstrasse 13
1070 Vienna
Tel: +43 664 1980 0401
www.jonasreindl.at

"We roast and brew with the goal of extracting the full potential of the coffee in your cup; that is how we honour the hard labor that was put in before us at the farm level."

Julias Meinl
Est. 1862 by Julias Meinl
Julius Meinl Gasse 3-7
1160 Vienna
Tel: +43 488 60 1311
www.meinl.com

"We traditionally blend our coffees from highland Arabica beans and quality Robustas grown in … Central and South America, East Africa, Ethiopia, India, and Papua New Guinea."

Rauwolf
Est. 2014 by Sandra and Michael Parzefall
Breitenfurter Str. 372
1230 Vienna
Tel: +43 660 661 7741
www.rauwolf-coffee.at

"We are always looking for extraordinary coffees that inspire us! We know where our coffee comes from and who works for us. We prefer to roast beans from small farms."

BELGIUM

Belgians have loved their coffee for hundreds of years, considering it something of a spiritual experience, inducing both a sense of contemplation as well as hospitality. They also like to partake in it along with something sweet like a small cake or biscuit. No wonder today coffee is their second-highest import!

Caffénation
Est.2003 by Rob Berghmans
Lamorinierestraat 161
2018 Antwerpen
Tel: +32 3 501 22 92
www.caffenation.be

"We are an artisanal specialty coffee roastery, meaning….light roast, fruity flavors, in-season beans, traceability, and transparent pricing. We dream, smell, and talk coffee night and day."

Madmum
Est.2018 by Pieter Claes
Tiensestraat 38
3000 Leuven
Tel: +32 470 79 32 32
www.madmumcoffee.be

"We aim for a more sustainable and ecological food chain. Therefore, we work with local suppliers, which results in a fresh, high quality and very tasty menu."

Maeskes Roem
Est.1925 by the Maes Family
Current owner: Callebaut-De Plecker family
Kortenbosdries 10
9310 Aalst
Tel: +32 53 70 17 51
www.maeskesroem.be

"Maeskes Roem has invested in a fully auto-mated packaging line, which allowed production to be increased, but never theless not to lose sight of the artisanal roasting of the coffee."

"Coffee is always a good idea."
– Anonymous

www.grahamescoffeeguide.com

MOK Coffee

Est.1992 by Jens Crabbé
Antoine Dansaertstraat 196
1000 Brussels
Tel: +32 495 31 67 18
www.mokcoffee.be

"We roast in small batches [which] allows us to fully control the roasting process, making sure that the tasting profile of the bean is just right…We always know the origin of the coffee beans."

Or Coffee

Est. 2000 by Tom Janssen and Katrien Pauwels
Dorpstraat 31
9230 Westrem
Tel: +32 9 336 3736
www.orcoffee.be

At Or, we only work with quality specialty Arabic coffee [and] a light roasting process, in which the bean keeps most of its natural aroma, is the only we can serve a coffee at its best."

BULGARIA

Dabov

Est.2008 by Jordan Dabov
58 Luben Karavelov Str.
Sofia 1142
Tel: +35 988 247 7000
www.dabov.coffee

"We choose farms that really care for the quality of their green beans…. We roast our coffees in one of the best roasting machines…. [our] coffees are packed in three-layer aluminum foil with the lowest possible permeability."

CROATIA

Cogito

Est. 2014 by Hannah and Matija Belkovic
Prilaz Gjure Deželića 40
10000 Zagreb
www.cogitocoffee.com

"We care about the quality of each batch we roast and each cup we serve. We source our coffee with care, emphasizing its seasonality and origin."

www.grahamescoffeeguide.com

"Pouring the Morning Coffee" by Laurits Tuxen (1906)

CYPRUS

Rich Coffee
Est.1948 by Michalis Nicolaides
Ellados 53
3041 Limassol
Tel: +357 257 62999
www.richcoffee.com
FT ☕ S 🌿

"Our aim is … for people to enjoy and learn the greatness of coffee from its origin to their cup and to realize that good coffee doesn't need to be an expensive one."

CZECH REPUBLIC

Doubleshot
Est. 2009 by Yara Tucek, Kamila Sotonova, and Jarda Hrstka
Debtary 37
250 91 Zelenec v Cechach
Tel: 420 314 004 550
www.doubleshot.cz

"A coffee roastery, three coffee shops, a training centre, a pastry shop but first and foremost, a team of people who love the world of specialty coffee. We have been living coffee."

Frolikova Kava
Est. 1992 by Petr Frolik
Jiráskova 555
Borohrádek, 517 24
Tel: 420 494 381 336
www.frolikovakava.cz

"Frolík´s coffee offers six kinds of blends … each [with] its own specific aroma and flavour. Their common features are a unique way of roasting and premium quality of used raw materials."

DENMARK

Denmark is consistently ranked among the happiest nations on Earth. Could it have something to do with the coffee? Well, it's true that Danes are also among the world's most prolific coffee drinkers. They consider their cafes a kind of oasis from the hubbub of the world to gather with friends for a warm drink and a good chat.

Coffee Collective
Est.2007 by Peter Dupont, Klaus Thomsen, Casper Rasmussen
Godthåbsvej 34B
2000 Frederiksberg
Tel: +45 60 15 15 25
www.coffeecollective.dk

"We wish to prove coffee a product of nature – of cultivation, varieties of coffee trees, soil conditions, rain, sun, wind – everything that in the end leave their distinct fingerprints on coffee's taste."

Merrild

Est.1964 by Moller Merrild
Erritsø Møllebanke 3
7000 Fredericia
Tel: +45 63 103 103
www.merrild-kaffe.dk

"Moths Merrild...did not think that the coffee products he found were good enough. He therefore began to roast coffee beans himself.... To this day you can still find all the original blends...."

Peter Larsen

Est.1902 by Peter Larsen
Ærøvej 15-17
8800 Viborg
Tel: +45 8662 6733
www.peterlarsenkaffe.dk
☕ C

"It is said that exercise makes mastery....But a long life has also taught us that passion trumps experience. If one wants to do one thing well, it requires a spark.... Especially when toasting coffee."

"Three Girls at the Children's Coffee" by Pietronella Peters

FINLAND

Perhaps it's the cold weather that causes Finns to drink more coffee in the world than any other country. Over the course of one year, the average Finn will drink 12kg of coffee. That's just over twice as much as Canadians who still rank 10th globally. Their enduring love of coffee has led this Nordic nation to produce some of the finest brews anywhere as you'll see below:

Good Life Coffee
Est.2012 by Lauri Pipinen
Kolmas linja 17
00530 Helsinki
Tel: +358 50 3808961
www.goodlifecoffee.fi

"We build our roasting profiles according to each bean to get the most out of the quality we've selected. Analytical, diligent and passionate, down to the nitty gritty. The way we see it, life's too short for weak coffee."

La Torrefazione
Est.2009 by Jens Hampf
Aleksanterinkatu 50
00100 Helsinki
Tel: +358 9 42890648
www.latorre.fi

"Even though the coffee is the most important thing to us, we try not to make it too complicated. In Finnish culture, coffee is often associated with taking a break and this is how it should be."

Mokkamestarit
Est.1990 by Reija Paakkinen and Mika Hannuniemi
Kuukuja 8E
33420 Tampere
Tel: +358 3 2530 145
www.mokkamestarit.fi

"An important part of our coffee range is female farmed coffee. Women are often in the weakest position in coffee production….By purchasing their products, we can support women's empowerment."

Paulig

Est.1876 by Gustav Paulig
Oy Gustav Paulig Ab
PB 15, 00981 Helsinki
Tel: +358 9 319 81
www.pauligshop.com
Ⓜ Ⓓ 🍃 FT

"Coffee is fine and delicate, which is why we take it passionately. Our selection always includes a wide range of high quality coffee flavours. At the Kulma shop, you can also buy freshly roasted coffee beans to take home."

"Seated Woman with Coffee" by Alphonse Mucha (c.1900)

FRANCE

What would a Parisian café be without coffee? The French nation can thank Suleyman Aga, the Ottoman Empire's ambassador to King Louis XIV, for bringing sacks of coffee with him to his post in 1669. Two years later, an Armenian named Pascal opened France's first café – and the rest, as they say, is history!

Belleville
Est.2013 by David Nigel Flynn
14b rue Lally Tollendal
75019 Paris
Tel: +33 1 01 86 76 09 58
www.cafesbelleville.com

"We are committed to… our exporters, importers and producers… illustrated year after year during visits to Honduras, Guatemala, Costa Rica, Kenya, Rwanda …to taste the new harvests."

Coutume
Est.2010 by Antoine Netien and Tom Clark
47 Rue de Babylone
75007 Paris
Tel: +33 185 081 867
www.coutumecafe.com
S

"We pay attention to all stages of coffee making: from plantation to cup. The selected green coffees come from five continents… are then roasted to… reveal the best of the aromatic identities unique to each."

Lomi
Est. 2010 by Paul Arnephy and Aleaume Paturle
3ter rue Marcadet
75018 Paris
Tel: +33 9 51 27 46 31
www.lomi.paris
 S

"Lomi roasts specialty coffees in an artisanal way sourced directly from producers. The know-how of our roaster Paul Arnephy has been rewarded with the title of Meilleur."

Terres de Cafe
Est. 2009 by Chris. Servell
6, R. des Blancs-Manteaux
Paris, Île-de-France 75004
Tel: +33 9 87 02 51 76
www.terresdecafe.com
S

"[We] offer a French-style interpretation of what coffee should be, built on the… principles of gastronomy, richness and knowledge of the terroirs, respect for the product, freshness and flavor."

Verlet

Est.1880 by Auguste Verlet
256 Rue St. Honore
75001 Paris
Tel: +33 1 42 60 67 39
www.verlet.fr
S ⌞C

"Our coffee roaster seeks out exceptional plantations producing delectable vintages in Colombia, Panama, and Guatemala, but also new, lesser-known plantations which Verlet fosters."

"Everyone should believe in something.
I believe I will have another coffee."
-- Anonymous

GERMANY

Mention German drinking and most people will think of beer. But in fact, on average, Germans drink 150 liters of coffee per year - more than beer, wine or mineral water. In fact, coffee is so beloved here that famed composer Johann Sebastian Bach honored the beverage with his "Coffee Cantata."

Barn, The

Est.2010 by Ralf Rueller
Schönhauser Allee 8
10119 Berlin
Tel: +49 163 8361605
www.thebarn.de

"We promise our farmers never to blend their coffees with others, and we keep our roasts light. By doing so, we can showcase terroir and the flavor profiles unique to each coffee farm."

Bonanza

Est.200 by Yumi Choi and Kiduk Reus
Orderberger Strasse 35
10435 Berlin
Tel: +49 30 208 488020
www.bonanzacoffee.de
S ⌞C

"We roast ... as little as possible, enough to fully develop all flavours, with the aim to highlight what makes a coffee distinct. The resulting cup should be clean, clear and pure."

www.grahamescoffeeguide.com

Five Elephant
Est.2010 by Kris and Sophie Schakman
Reichenberger Str. 101
10999 Berlin
Tel: +49 30 284 84320
www.fiveelephant.com
S

"Passionate about quality, our goal is to source the best coffees in the world in a way that is mindful of our environmental impact and thoughtful of the social impact of the communities who produce our coffees."

Hoppenworth & Ploch
Est.2008 by Julian Ploch & Matthias Hoppenworth
Friedberger Landstraße 86
60316 Frankfurt
Tel: +49 69/84779249
www.hoppenworth-ploch.de
S

"We have mainly dedicated ourselves to the light roasts, because these make the full complexity of the different origins tangible. But we also have a selection of darker roasts."

Man vs. Machine
Est.2014 by Marco Mehrwald
Müllerstrasse 23
80469 Munich
Tel: +49 89 54847777
www.mvsm.coffee
S

"We are 100% independent …We roast nothing but the highest grade Arabica Coffees (Specialty Grade >80pts.) Our main focus, always is and always will be quality before growth."

GREECE

Coffee Island
Est.2009 by Evangelos Liolios
30 Vrisakion Street Patras
263 34
Tel: +30 2610 643 679
www.coffeeisland.gr
 S C

"Weve been roasting coffee for more than a decade…. we use our knowledge, experience, skills and love of coffee to give the beans their best flavor and aroma."

"The Coffee Bearer"
by John Frederick Lewis (1857)

HUNGARY

Blue Bird
Est.2013 by Alex Aizelman
Rumbach Sebestyén u. 12
1075 Budapest
Tel: +36 30 784 9081
www.bluebirdcafe.eu
Ⓛ Ⓜ Ⓓ S 🌿 ☕

"In our grinder we put always fresh and best quality beans….We roast our coffee with great care and carefully experimented method to maximize the enjoyment of the different flavors from different areas."

ICELAND

Reykjavik Roasters
Est.2008 by Torfi Þór Torfason
Brautarholt 2
Reykjavík
Tel: +354 552 3200
www.reykjavikroasters.is

"A lot of work goes into every cup you taste….Every batch of beans is carefully studied and roasted trying different profiles until we find the one that highlights to perfection the best qualities of the beans."

"Scene at a Café in Cairo, Eygp, 18th Century"

IRELAND

Just as in the rest of Europe, coffee was introduced to Ireland in the 1600s. Coffee houses soon followed, springing up around the country, and becoming a way of life. Today, Irish baristas have achieved distinction in global competitions and established renowned roasteries like some of those below:

Ariosa Coffee
Est. 2003 by Michael Kelly
Borronstown Ashbourne
County Meath
Tel: +353 1 801 0962
www.ariosacoffee.com

"We buy directly…from growers ensuring that the care and passion that they take in producing speciality graded beans is emulated by us through our roasting method and delivery process."

Badger & Dodo
Est. 2008 by Brock Lewin
Fermore
County Cork
Tel: +353 85 706 2019
www.badgeranddodo.ie

"3rd wave coffee roasters roast in smaller roasters… because it allows much greater control over heat. We understand that heat needs to be tamed to bring out the unique characteristics of every crop."

Ponaire
Est. 2006 by Tommy and Jennifer Ryan
Main Street
Newport, Tipperary
Tel: + 353 61 373 712
www.ponaire.ie

"We import high quality Arabica beans from around the world and hand roast them to meticulously draw out unique flavors. We 'cup' all batches to ensure the highest quality."

Silverskin
Est. 2012 by Brian Kenny
Westlink Business Park
Kylemore Rd, D10 A062
Tel: + 353 087 9012700
www.silverskincoffee.ie

"Our coffee is craft-roasted daily in small batches to guarantee freshness and allow us to maintain strict quality control throughout the entire roasting process."

"Coffee in the Garden" by Daniel Ridgway Knight (c.1900)

ITALY

There's a reason Italy is considered the world's coffee capital: they simply make great coffee! Perhaps it helps that they got a headstart, becoming the first Europeans to import coffee, starting in the 16th Century. They also created the "espresso" which has since found a special place in the hearts of coffee drinkers worldwide.

Caffé Vergnano
Est.1882 by Domenico Vergnano
C. Vittorio Emanuele II, 44
10123 Torino
Tel: +39 011 882 2400
www.caffevergnano.com

"For over 135 years, Caffè Vergnano has been telling the ritual of espresso, enhancing every aspect while preserving the craftsmanship transmitted by Domenico Vergnano."

Ditta Artigianale
Est.2013 by Francesco Sanapo and Patrick Hoffer
Via dei Neri 32
50122 Florence
Tel: +39 055 274 1541
www.dittaartigianale.it
S

"After years of research and study around the world, on the different systems and ways of understanding coffee, [we] dreamed of applying this phenomenon of specialty coffee in the Italian market."

Filicori Zecchini
Est.1919 by Aldo Filicori and Luigi Zecchini
Via delle Lame
44 40122 Bologna
Tel: +39 051 484 1029
www.filicorizecchini.com
(M) (D)

"For years, the company has chosen to carry out separate roasting for each of its single-origin coffees, because every type of green coffee has its own optimum roasting time…to obtain the best flavor."

Gardelli
Est.2010 by Rubens Gardelli
Via Balzella 28/A
47121 Forlì FC
Tel: +39 0543 721136
www.gardellicoffee.com
S DC

"We are committed to selecting the coffee of the best quality….only the mature cherries….we roast three times a week only specific coffees in the quantity ordered, and we ship them the same day."

Sciascia
Est.1919 by Adolpho Sciascia
Via Fabio Massimo 80
00192 Rome
Tel: +39 06 3211580
www.sciasciacaffe1919.it

"The goal of Sciascia is to offer only the best…not only unique but in a wide range of flavors…coffee with dark chocolate, great cappuccino, coffee cream, Sicilian red orange granitas, Ciaculli mandarins, Amalfi lemons."

"I'm a coffee fanatic. Once you go to proper coffee, you can't go back. You cannot go back." – Hugh Laurie

---

LITHUANIA

Taste Map
Est. 2011 by Domas and
Leva Ivonis
M. K. Čiurlionio g. 8
LT-03104 Vilnius
Tel: +370 629 29 136
www.tastemap.lt
S D 🌿

"Much more than roasting coffee beans and preparing coffee, we create and cherish coffee culture – inspiring, comprehensible and accessible to everyone."

LUXEMBOURG

Knopes
Est. 1936 by Albert Knopes
Ave. de la Porte Neuve
Luxembourg City 2227
Tel: +352 26 27 06 26
www.knopes.com
🌿 S

"To roast using the traditional craft method…is a family story here. Fabien Knopes, 4th generation of roasters, continues the search for perfection and the selection of the best coffees."

"Girl Drinking Coffee" by Albert Anker (1910)

NETHERLANDS

Dutch traders played a key, early role in spreading coffee, becoming the largest supplier in Europe and also bringing coffee plants to India and Indonesia. Thanks to those long sea voyages, they also created the cold brewing method, which preserves coffee longer.

Back to Black
Est.2015 by Noortje Vlutters and Inge Bulthuis
Weteringstraat 48
1017 SP Amsterdam
Tel: 020-3044988
www.backtoblackcoffee.nl
S

"We are constantly looking for exceptional coffees with outspoken characteristics to thereafter roast this coffee in the best possible way. We carefully select the green bean importers of our coffee."

Bocca
Est. 2003 by Menno and Tewis Simons
Kerkstraat 96H
1017 GP Amsterdam
Tel: 31 32 313 46 67
www.bocca.nl
S 🄳 🌿

"We manage the entire bean-to-cup process: from sourcing to roasting and packaging to serving….Our roasters know exactly how to bring the best out of every bean – that ideal ratio of sweetness to acidity."

Drupa
Est. 2018 by Martin and Cristina Amadio
E. Anjeliersdswardstraat 16
1015 NR, Amsterdam
Tel: 31 828 777 4861
www.drupacoffee.com
☕ S

"[We] focus on Colombian coffee…. Our coffees come from micro-lots and small producers, through a sustainable process from the farm to the cup. We believe in collaborating."

White Label
Est. 2014 by Francesco Grassotti and Elmer Oomkens
Jan Evertsenstraat 136
1056 EK Amsterdam
Tel: 31 20 737 1359
www.whitelabelcoffee.nl
S

"We roast coffee to highlight its natural diversity….We focus on quality, openness and cooperation all through the chain…. we are always open for new partners and projects."

NORWAY

You don't get to be the second-highest consuming nation of coffee drinkers per capita without knowing a thing or two about how to make an excellent brew. Norwegians are known to prefer a lighter roast, which they say reveals more of the bean's aromas. They tend also to drink it throughout the day – which, during their summers, can be quite long!

Stockfleths
Est.1895 by Astri Stockfleths
Karl Johans gate 25
0159 Oslo
Tel: +47 40 092361
www.stockfleths.as

"We love the work behind giving you a good taste experience…. everything we offer must be of the highest quality. Our focus is on constantly improving and developing ourselves."

Supreme Roastworks
Est.2007 by Magnus Lindskog and Joar Christoffersen
Thorvald Meyers gate 18
0555 Oslo
Tel: +47 22 71 4202
www.srw.no

"We love serving our amazing customers and working with people who truly enjoy and understand our concept and philosophy. As we like to say: no fuss–just great coffee."

Tim Wendelboe
Est. 2007 by Tim Wendelboe
Grüners gate 1
0552 Oslo
Tel: +47 944 31 627
www.timwendelboe.no
S

"We are known for our light-roasted coffees and our focus on transparency and longterm work for improving coffee quality with the coffee producers we buy from. We roast to order."

"Sometimes I go hours without drinking coffee. It's called sleeping."
       -- Anonymous

"Peasant Girl Drinking Coffee" by Camille Pissarro (1881)

POLAND

Coffee Proficiency
Est. 2014 by Lukasz Jura
a. 29 Listopada 155c
31-406 Kraków
Tel: +48 733 984 688
www.coffeeproficiency.com
S

"Our best coffees come from direct trade…from carefully selected plantations. When the beans reach Kraków, we roast them in our laboratory accordingly to the profile adapted to their individual characteristics."

PORTUGAL

Booinga
Est.2011 by Carlos Vieira
R. M. de Albuquerque 449
4450-206 Matosinhos
Tel: +351 968 804 435
www.booinga.com

"Booínga was created to offer coffee lovers products of exceptional quality.... When possible, we choose organic coffees...to insure that the production is being made sustainably."

Combi
Est.2014 by G. Gonzy, F. Cardoso, and J. Avilar
Morgado de Mateus nº29
4000-234 Porto
Tel: +351 929 444 939
www.combi-coffee.com

"It all started with a van that brought specialty coffee to various stops including festivals....[now] Combi is a fixed space...and also a factory where green beans are roasted."

Delta Cafes
Est.1961 by Azinhais Nabeiro
Rua das Flores 63
1200-193 Lisboa
Tel: +351 268 009 200
www.deltacafes.com

"Well versed in the coffee market...Rui Nabeiro decided to create his own brand...in a small warehouse with 50 square metres of space and without many resources, activity started with just two small roasters."

Fabrica
Est. 2015 by Stanislav Benderski
Av. Calouste Gulbenkian 15
Campo Maior
Tel: +351 21 139 2948
fabricacoffeeroasters.com

"We carefully roast our beans according to their characteristics and purpose – light roast for filter coffee or a slightly darker roast for espresso, and so ensuring the extraordinary results we always aim to achieve."

"Laurette with a Cup of Coffee" by Henri Matisse (1917)

SLOVAKIA

Sweet Beans
Est. 2005 by Jan Krekan
Obchodná 37/b
811 06 Bratislava
Tel: +421 902 466 584
www.sweetbeans.coffee
S

"Sweet is a very desirable descriptor when it comes to coffee evaluation….That's why we were very excited to use this word in our name to identify ourselves… hopefully you would feel it in your cup."

SPAIN

Originally introduced by Arab traders, coffee drinking has become deeply embedded into Spanish culture. Typically, Spaniards will start their day with a *café con leche* – a strong, black coffee mixed with hot milk. In contrast to many northern Europeans, Spaniards often prefer a dark roast. In the evening, they might top off their coffee with a bit of rum, known as a *carajillo*.

El Magnifico
Est.1962 by the Velasco Family
Argentería 64
08003 Barcelona
Tel: +34 93 319 39 75
www.cafeselmagnifico.com
S ℃

"We roast a carefully selected choice of fine coffees, until today…. Coffee is one of the most complex aromatic and gustatory things that the human being ingests."

D'Origen
Est.2012 by Marco and Michael Uhlig
Partida Cap Blanch, 73
03590 Altea (Alicante)
Tel: 966 10 43 85
www.dorigencoffee.es
S ℃ 🌿

"We select specialty coffees from around the world, taking maximum care of the roast to extract the best from each origin. And we do it on the shores of the Mediterranean, on the Costa Blanca."

Hola Coffee
Est. 2016 by Nolo Botana and Pablo Caballero
Calle del Dr. Fourquet 33
28012 Madrid
Tel: +34 910 56 82 63
www.hola.coffee
☕ S ℃

"We roast specialty coffee beans weekly in Madrid… fresh seasonal coffees of different origins, light or developed roasts and…the option of grinding it at the point that best suits your coffee maker."

"Coffee is a hug in a mug."
　　　　　　　　　　　　-- Anonymous

---

www.grahamescoffeeguide.com

Nomad Coffee
Est.2014 by Jordi Mestre
Carrer de Pujades 95
08005 Barcelona
Tel: +34 628 566 235
www.nomadcoffee.es
S

"Week after week we work together to achieve the best results with our coffees….We roast, serve, distribute, train, play, experiment and advise…. It's important to us that you receive the best."

Right Side
Est.2012 by Joaquin Parra
Carrer de la Indústria 7
08860 Barcelona
Tel: +34 931 92 80 08
www.rightsidecoffee.com
S

"We are a small but solid, socially responsible team with one particular passion: to share with you extraordinary flavors. We want you to rediscover and really enjoy your daily cup of coffee."

SWEDEN

Drop
Est.2009 by Joanna Alm and Stephen Leighton
Wollmar Yxkullsgatan 10
118 50 Stockholm
Tel: +31 30 297 9111
www.dropcoffee.com
S

"We are roasting the coffee carefully with a total focus on the sweetness and vibrancy of every unique coffee, always striving for a clarity in the coffee, without ashy flavours."

Johan & Nystrom
Est.2004 by Johan Damgaard and Ben Gorham
Lyftkransvägen 11
142 50 Skogås
Tel: 46 8 530 22
www.ohanochnystrom.se
 S

"Our coffee is carefully selected by coffee farmers and friends who share our passion in quality. Our philosophy is based on the origin, the grower's knowledge, and full transparency.

SWITZERLAND

Mame
Est. 2016 by Emi Fukahori
and Mathieu Theis
Josefstrasse 160
8005 Zürich
Tel:
www.mame.coffee

"We like coffees with character. We roast to showcase the characters of each coffee. We choose to have a specific roast profile for each espresso and a specific roast profile for each filter coffee.

Valmandin
Est. 2015 by Neslihan Grasser
46 rue Ancienne
1227 Carouge, Geneva
Tel: +41 22 547 18 91
www.valmandin.ch

"We freshly roast our coffees in Switzerland, slowly, with a traditional method to obtain the right aromas….We select the best beans on seasonal availability, and only roast 100% Arabica.

"O.S. Tseytlin and D.V. Vysotsky at Coffee"
by Leonid Pasternik (1913)

UNITED KINGDOM

Introduced to England from Arabia in the 1600s, coffee was initially perceived as a medicinal product used for treating such ailments as headaches, gout, or drunkenness. However, the soothing black beverage soon became the centerpiece of English coffeehouses where friends could gather for a hot cup and the latest news. Today, UK's cutting-edge coffee roasters are helping to lead the way in producing award-winning brews appreciated globally.

Artisan Roast
Est. 2007 by Gustavo Pardo and Michael Wilson
57 Broughton Street EH1 3RJ Edinburgh
Tel: +44 7590 590667
www.artisanroast.co.uk
S

"We invest a huge amount of time and energy in sourcing great coffee and we make the quality of the beans is preserved when we roast….This means roasting every lot in a unique way…."

Caffé Nerro
Est.1997 by Gerry Ford
60-61 Trafalgar Square
London WC2N 5DS
Tel: +44 207 520 5150
www.caffenero.com
S C

"Making great coffee takes some doing. So, we built our own Roastery and created a unique award-winning coffee blend. We regularly work on developing new and interesting blends."

Caravan Coffee
Est.2010 by Miles Kirby, Laura Harper-Hinton, and Chris Ammermann
152 Great Portland Street
London W1W 6AJ
Tel: +44 203 963 8500
caravancoffeeroasters.co.uk
S

"From the day a new coffee arrives into our restaurants and take-out bars, we are thinking about the best way to showcase its individual character. We do this by continually evaluating our brewing methods."

Dr. Wakefield
Est.1970 by Derrick Wakefield
42 - 44 Dolben Street
London SE1 0UQ
Tel: 44 20 7202 2620
www.drwakefield.com
S ⅅ 🌿

"We have a strict process for checking the quality of all the green coffee we order both before and after it is shipped to us. We also buy from the same farmers and exporters year after year."

Origin
Est. 2005 by Tom Sobey
65 Charlotte Rd, Shoreditch
London, EC2A 3PE
Tel: 44 2077 296252
www.origincoffee.co.uk
☕ ⅅ

"Over the last 15 years, we've been exploring coffee. Seeking new flavours, collaborators and lessons in the pursuit of an exceptional cup."

United States and Canada

CANADA

With those brutally cold winters, it's no wonder that coffee has flourished in Canada, bringing forth such popular national chains as Tim Horton's (started, no surprise, by a Canadian hockey player). All in all, Canadians consume some 14 billions cups a year. That's a lot of brew. Perhaps their most distinctive coffee creation: maple-infused espresso!

National

Second Cup
Est.1975 by Tom Culligan and Frank O'Dea
6303 Airport Road
Mississauga, ON L4V 1R8
Tel: 855-379-3388
www.secondcup.com

"Our passion begins by choosing only the finest 100% Specialty Grade Arabica beans…. Our award-winning artisanal roaster processes the coffee in small batches to ensure the best flavor."

Tim Hortons
Est.1964 by Tim Horton and Ron Joyce
130 King Street West
Toronto, ON, M5X 1C9
Tel: 888-601-1616
www.timhortons.com

"Over the years, Tim Hortons has captured the hearts and taste buds of Canadians…. serving over 5 million cups of coffee every day with 80% of Canadians visiting a Tims in Canada at least once a month."

Van Houtte
Est.1919 by Albert-Louis Van Houtte
8300,19th Avenue
Montreal H1Z 4J8
Tel: 514 593-7711
www.vanhoutte.com

"We have sourced the finest Arabica beans from the same producers for decades….Upon arriving in Canada, the beans are subjected to a series of tests to assess their quality… Only the best beans are roasted."

Alberta

Phil & Sebastian

Est.2009 by Phil Robertson
and Sebastian Sztabzyb
18 Confluence Way SE,
Calgary, AB T2G 0G1
Tel: 587-353-2268
www.philsebastian.com
☕ ⓒ S

"This has always been a labour of love. We're engineers and coffee lovers first, and businesspeople second. Our focus…since day one [is] creating great coffee and sharing it with folks that appreciate it."

British Columbia

Milano

Est.1984 by Francesco
Curatolo. Current owner:
Brian Turko.
156 West 8th Avenue
Vancouver BC, V5Y 1N2
Tel: 604-8794468
www.milanocoffee.ca
☕ Ⓜ ⓒ 🌿

"Brian was born and raised in Vancouver's Little Italy. There he discovered espresso bars… including Café de Milano… Following his mentorship to Francesco, Brian continued to dedicate his life to the pursuit of the perfect blend."

Timbertrain

Est.2014 by Peter Kim, Jeff
Shin, and Min Shin
311 W Cordova St,
Vancouver, BC V6B 4K2
Tel: 604-915-9188
www.timbertraincoffee
roasters.com
☕ S ⓒ

"Timbertrain is dedicated in crafting precision into the flavor of every sip of coffee … to closely monitor the rigorous process that its coffee takes - from sourcing to roasting and experimenting."

Nova Scotia

Java Blend

Est.1938 by Theodore Sideris
6027 North Street
Halifax, NS B3K 1N9
Tel: 902-423-6944
www.javablendcoffee.com
☕ ☕ S ⓒ FT 🌿

"Direct from our roaster to your cup….We strive to delight our customers with coffees of unsurpassed quality, and in so doing to support some of the finest small farmers in the world."

Ontario

De Mello Palheta
Est.2013 by Felix and Won Ho Cha
2489 Yonge Street
Toronto, ON M4P 2H6
Tel: 647-748-3633
www.hellodemello.com

"De Mello Palheta offers an origin-based approach to coffee, procuring coffees from a large variety of regions and roasting to showcase the traits inherent of the terroir of these respective regions."

Pilot
Est.2009 by Andy and Jessie Wilkins
439 Richmond St West
M5V 1X9 Toronto
Tel: 416-393-6000
www.pilotcoffeeroasters.com

"All of our our coffees are specialty grade, which … means it has received a grading of 80-points or higher…. We love coffee, and appreciate the nuance of every bean."

Propeller
Est. 2013 by Losel Tethong
439 Richmond St West
M5V 1X9 Toronto
Tel: 416-393-6000
www.propellercoffee.com

"Each coffee is unique…. growing regions, growing conditions, bean densities & moisture content all contribute different taste…. We roast with the end goal of unlocking all of each coffee's full potential."

Quebec

Dispatch
Est. 2012 by Chrissy Durcak
267 Rue St. Zotique
Montreal, Quebec H3G 2H7
Tel: 514-504-2351
www.dispatchcoffee.ca

"Raising awareness and building a fairer, more transparent supply chain is our raison d'etre….We work with coffee farmers, importers, and partners across the globe."

Nektar

Est. 2009 by Guillaume Michaud
235 St-Joseph Est
Québec, QC, G1K 3B1
Tel: 418 977-9236
www.nektar.ca

S DC

"Coffee involves millions of people…Here's our mission: the best selection of coffees on the market; encourage people to discover and learn about coffee; help producers to become known for their work."

"The Coffee Drinker" by Ivana Kobilca (1888)

UNITED STATES

It is said that Capt. John Smith, founder of the Virginia Colony, brought the first coffee to America in 1607 after discovering it during his travels in Turkey. By the mid-1700s, coffee could be had in most taverns. But it was thanks to the Boston Tea Party which saw Colonists dumping tea in the harbor as a protest against British taxation that coffee really took off. And it's never looked back. Today, coffee in the U.S. is a $36 billion industry with 31,000 coffee shops, 280 million cups served daily, and some incredibly innovative coffee.

National

Chock full o'Nuts
Est.1926 by Charles Black
1370 Progress Road
Suffolk, VA 23434
www.chockfullonuts.com
Tel: 888-246-2598
Ⓓ Ⓜ Ⓛ S ㏅

"After the Great Depression, William Black switched from roasting nuts to roasting coffee beans and…begins to sell the coffee in grocery stores across New York. He names it after his original shop."

Dunn Brothers
Est.1987 by Ed and Dan Dunn
111 Third Avenue South
Minneapolis, MN 55401
Tel: 612-334-9746
www.dunnbrothers.com
Ⓓ Ⓜ Ⓛ ☕ ㏅

"We roast small batches of coffee, in-store, every day. That's why our coffee is never more than 5 days old. Roasting in small batches promises a more fresh, rich, and enjoyable coffee experience."

Folger's
Est.1892 by James Folger
Current owner: J.M.Smucker
1 Strawberry Lane
Orrville, Ohio 44667-0280
www.folgerscoffee.com
Tel: 800-937-9745
☕ Ⓓ Ⓜ Ⓛ ㏅

"While many coffee importers…bought and sold beans based on appearance, the idea of 'cup-testing' was born in San Francisco. James implemented this technique and began cup-testing shipments of beans himself."

www.grahamescoffeeguide.com

Maxwell House

Est.1892 by Joel Owsley Cheek
200 E Randolph St #7600,
Chicago, IL 60601
Tel: 800-543-5335
www.maxwellhouse.com

"Good to the last drop, one cup at a time…Each blend is selected from five different types of beans… custom-roasted for a perfectly balanced taste."

Peet's Coffee and Tea

Est.1966 by Alfred Peet
1400 Park Ave.
Emeryville, CA 94608
Tel: 800-999-2132
www.peets.com

"We use our five senses—not computers—to unlock each bean's flavor potential. Our roasters are masters of their craft, fine-tuning the nuances of each blend and single origin they roast."

Stumptown Coffee

Est. 1999 by Duane Sorenson
100 SE Salmon Street
Portland, OR 97214
Tel: 855-711-3385
www.stumptowncoffee.com

"Roast just enough to bring out the best and full potential of what's inherent in each particular coffee…to draw out things like acidity, floral notes, chocolate, molasses, and earth. All of the coffee's flavor potentials are presented at the first crack."

Alabama

Red Diamond

Est.1906 by William Donovan
400 Park Avenue
Moody, AL 35004
Tel: 800-292-4651
www.reddiamond.com

"We always select new crop coffee beans…to create a sweet rich flavor and aroma…. Our Scolari Roasters are the finest in the world, imported from Italy."

Revelator

Est.2014 by J. Owen, E. Chevalier, and E. Pogue
1826 3rd Avenue North
Birmingham, AL 35203
Tel: 205-224-5900
www.revelatorcoffee.com

"We source seasonally, keeping our menu fluid, and choose expressive coffees that showcase variety and region. Our offerings are simple and our menu is intentional."

Alaska

Alaska Artisan Coffee
Est.1996 by Ron Maclure
4576 S. Glenn Highway
Palmer, AK 99645
Tel: 907-745-5543
alaskaartisancoffee.com
Ⓓ Ⓜ Ⓛ D꜀

"Ron is not your average roaster. He strives to offer not only the freshest coffee blends, but the most unique coffee experience you'll ever have....Our roasting facility is located in beautiful Palmer."

Alaska Coffee Roasting
Est.1994 by Michael Gesser
4001 Geist Road
Fairbanks, AK 99709
Tel: 907-457-5282
alaskacoffeeroasting.com
☕ ☕

"We specialize in single estate varietal coffee beans, and like fine wine, each batch is tasted and approved before receiving the ACRC seal of approval."

"At The Coffee Table" by Edvard Munch (1883)

Arizona

Press Coffee
Est.2008 by Steve Kraus and Tram Mai
10443 N. 32nd Street
Phoenix, AZ 85028
Tel: 602-314-4201
www.presscoffee.com

"10 years and 8 valley locations later, Press Coffee has become an Arizona staple among specialty coffee enthusiasts while earning national recognition for their coffees. "

Arkansas

Onyx Coffee Lab
Est.2012 by Jon/Andrea Allen
2418 N. Gregg Ave.
Fayetteville, AR 72701
Tel: 479-444-6557
www.onyxcoffeelab.com

"It all starts with the green coffee. We believe that no amount of roasting expertise …can take the place of the kind of green coffee that's the result of intentionality at the farm level."

California

Blue Bottle
Est.2002 by James Freeman
476 9th Street
Oakland, CA 94607
Tel: 510-653-3394
www.bluebottlecoffee.com
FT

"We taste each coffee to determine the precise days on which it will achieve peak flavor. We only serve the absolute freshest coffee to you in our cafes and on our webshop."

Coffee Bean & Tea Leaf, The
Est.1963 by Herb Hyman
5700 Wilshire Blvd.
Los Angeles, CA 90036
Tel: 310-237-2326
www.coffeebean.com

"We roast in small batches at our facility in Camarillo, where we find the roast that best suits the beans from each origin and captures what makes each country's coffee unique."

Equator Coffee
Est.1995 by Brooke McDonnell and Helen Russell
115 Jordan Street
San Rafael, CA 94901
Tel: 800-809-7687
www.equatorcoffees.com

"Equator's dedicated and experienced roasting team transform the farmers' efforts into the raw materials needed to prepare the highest quality cup of coffee."

LA Mill
Est.1991 by Craig Min
1636 Silver Lake Blvd
Los Angeles, CA 90026
Tel: 626-202-0100
www.lamillcoffee.com

We source from the finest coffee and tea producing estates and regions in the world. Less than 1% of all coffee beans and tea leaves produced annually meet our exacting standards.

Philz Coffee
Est.1978 by Phil Jaber
4101 24th Street
San Francisco, CA 94110
Tel: 415-875-9370
www.philzcoffee.com

"You won't find any lattes, cappuccinos, espressos, or pre-brews. Instead, you'll find over 20 customized blends made from high quality beans from around the world."

Verve
Est.2007 by Colby Barr and Ryan O'Donovan
104 Bronson Street
Santa Craz, CA 95062
Tel: 831-464-8141
www.vervecoffee.com

"Verve came to be through the serendipitous union of surf, sweat and a love of life and living…. our roots remain planted in Santa Cruz, where we roast our coffee on vintage roasters."

Colorado

Huckleberry
Est.2011 by Koan Goedman and Mark Mann
4301 Pecos Street
Denver, CO 80211
Tel: 866-558-2201
huckleberryroasters.com

"We are committed to building a sustainable business that prioritizes working with smallholder farms and coffee co-ops. More generally, we seek to be a responsible business…."

GRAHAME'S COFFEE GUIDE

Sweet Bloom
Est.2013 by Andy Sprenger
1619 N. Reed St.
Lakewookd, CO 80214
Tel: 303-261-5954
sweetbloomcoffee.com
S

"All coffee begins with a bloom: an elegant, fragrant white flower. Exceptional coffee, freshly roasted and ground, blooms again when infused with hot water - equally fragrant and even more complex."

District of Columbia

Swing's Coffee
Est.1916 by Michael Swing
640 14th Street, NW
Washington, DC 20005
Tel: 202-652-0188
www.swingscoffee.com
☕ ⅅℂ S

"We roast ethically-sourced coffees behind a glass wall....our transparency applies to both sourcing and roasting. Always, we are eager to share our craft and coffee discoveries."

"Portrait of Nephew" by Antoni Piotrowski (1837)

www.grahamescoffeeguide.com

Florida

Eternity Coffee
Est. 2011 by Chris Johnson, Ernesto and Cristina Garces
117 SE 2nd Avenue
Miami, FL 33131
Tel: 305-350-7761
www.eternitycoffee
roasters.com

"Along with our unique Colombian estate farms and micro-lots, we source green coffees from around the globe….artisanally roasted by a master roaster in small batches, we maintain a quality and transparency…"

Panther Coffee
Est.2010 by Letitia and Michael Pollock
5934 NW 2nd Ave
Miami, FL 33127
Tel: 305-677-3952
www.panthercoffee.com
S

"After the selection of green coffee, the roasting team defines the specific roast profile to be used. Their goal is to achieve full development and caramelization of the sugars present within the coffee bean."

Georgia

Jittery Joe's
Est.1994 by ?
425 Barber Street
Atherns, GA 30601
Tel: 877-438-5637
www.jitteryjoes.com

"We roast in small batches to allow for greater quality and care. This process allows us to be intimately involved in every roasting batch to ensure you're getting the best cup of coffee possible."

Hawaii

Big Island Coffee Roasters
Est.2010 by B. Von Damitz
16-1193 Uhini Ana Rd.
Mountain View, HI 96771
Tel: 808-968-6228
bigislandcoffeeroasters.com

"Our farm and roasting company grew from a penchant to explore our senses….With attention and taste, we weave the best coffees from Hawaii's wild and beautiful places with fine craftsmanship and display."

Hawaiian Island Kona Coffee

Est. 1981 by Michael Boulware
2839 Makumoa Street
Honolulu, HI 96819
Tel: 800-657-7716
www.hawaiianisles.com
Ⓓ Ⓜ S

"[We are] a 2nd generation, family-owned coffee roaster located in the heart of the Hawaiian Islands. We aim to share the unique taste of Hawaii with the world through …our custom coffees."

Koa Coffee

Est. 1997 by Marin Artukovich
1560 Hart Street
Honolulu, HI
Tel: 866-562-5282
www.koacoffee.com
Ⓓ Ⓜ S

"We pick every bean by hand, harvesting only when the beans are cherry red. No mechanical harvesting that would mix bitter green beans in with the red. We have real people roasting your coffee."

Illinois

Big Shoulders Coffee

Est. 2012 by Tim Coonan
1948 West Lake Street
Chicago, Ill. 606012
Tel: 312-846-1883
bigshoulderscoffee.com
S 🌱 FT

"Beans are sourced from farmers we have grown relationships with and roasted specifically to preserve the integrity … of the coffee. We brew the coffee with down-to-the-second precision."

Intelligentsia Coffee

Est. 1995 by Doug Zell and Emily Mange
1850 W. Fulton Street
Chicago, Ill. 60612
Tel: 312-563-0023
www.intelligentsiacoffee.com
☕ S Ⓓ C

"Intelligentsia single-origin coffees are sourced from some of the most decorated estates, family-owned farms, and farmer organizations…. Each one represents a unique expression of flavor."

"Coffee – the favorite drink of the civilized world." — *Thomas Jefferson*

---

www.grahamescoffeeguide.com

Kansas

PT's Coffee
Est.1993 by Jeff Taylor and Fred Polzin
1635 SW Washburn Ave.
Topeka, KS 66604
Tel: 785-862-5282
www.ptscoffee.com
Ⓓ Ⓜ ☕ S

"Exceptional coffee depends upon great partnerships, and our partners are selected for more than just their harvests— they are socially responsible and environmentally conscious."

Kentucky

Quills Coffee
Est.2007 by Nathan Quillo
930 Baxter Avenue
Louisville, KY 40204
Tel: 502-742-6129
www.quillscoffee.com
☕ 🕮 S

"Quills was born to create a space where … coffee lovers in Louisville could fuel their passion…. We want to get your coffees as fresh as possible…. Currently we do all our production roasting on Monday and Tuesday."

"Farmhouse Activities" by Gottfried Mind (c.1800)

Louisiana

Community Coffee
Est.1919 by "Cap" Saurage
3332 Partridge Lane, Bldg A
Baton Rouge, LA 70809
Tel: 800-884-5282
www.communitycoffee.com

"Our experts are focused on making rich, bold and flavorful coffee, and our ground and whole bean coffee is constantly monitored with quality check points for brewing, aroma and taste."

Maine

Coffee By Design
Est.1994 by May Allen Lindemann and Alan Spear
1 Diamond Street
Portland, ME 04101
Tel: 207-874-5400
www.coffeebydesign.com

"We search for…only the top 1% of Arabica coffee beans that are picked and sorted by hand…. Before we select which beans to roast, we extensively research and sample the product."

Maryland

Dublin Coffee Roasters
Est.1999 by Seirna Roy
1780 N. Market Street
Baltimore, MD 21701
Tel: 240-674-1740
dublincoffeeroasters.com

"Serina sources raw coffee beans from small farms in countries such as Columbia, India, Ecuador, Vietnam, Brazil, Honduras, and Guatemala. Our roasting facility…is always open for visitors."

"Without coffee, nothing gets written. Period." – writer Nancy Kress

Massachusetts

George Howell
Est.2004 by Gearage Howell
312 School Street
Acton, MA 01720
Tel: 866-444-5282
georgehowellcoffee.com

"Our coffee is craft-roasted daily in small batches to guarantee freshness…. Once our quality control group has approved a batch, it is packaged immediately in airtight, one-way valve bags."

New England Coffee
Est. 1916 by Menelaos and George Kaloyanides, Megaklis Papadopoulos
100 Charles Street
Malden, MA 02148
Tel: 800-225-3537
www.newenglandcoffee.com

"Each variety of bean requires a different roast time and our experienced roasters use smell and sight to determine when the desired roast has been achieved….There's no substitute for experience."

Shelburne Falls
Est. 1990 by Kathy Lytle and Curtis Rich
1335 Mohawk Trail
Shelburne Falls, MA 01370
shelburnefallscoffee.com

"Nestled in the foothills of New England's Berkshires, our coffee roastery hearkens back to an earlier America…our hand roasted coffee beans….are as delicious as coffee can be."

Michigan

Coffee Beanery
Est.1976 by Joanne and Julius Shaw
3429 Pierson Place
Flushing, MI 48433
Tel: 800-441-2255
www.coffeebeanery.com

"You can sense the difference the moment you arrive at our 45,000 square-foot facility… where all of our hand-selected beans are roasted, flavored and packaged…The abundant aroma of fresh roasted coffee surrounds you."

GRAHAME'S COFFEE GUIDE

Madcap Coffee
Est.2008 by Trevor Corlett and Ryan Knapp
98 Monroe Center NW
Grand Rapids, MI 49503
Tel: 888-866-9091
www.madcapcoffee.com

"Every year, we taste thousands of coffees and only select the few that we find truly special....Much of our year is spent out of the country, exploring our favorite regions, visiting our partners and investigating their land."

"Girl with Breakfast Tray" by Marcin Jablonski (1875)

Minnesota

Dogwood Coffee
Est. 2010 by Dan Anderson and Greg Hoyt
1209 Tyler Street NE
Minneapolis, MN 55413
Tel: 612-202-8986
www.dogwoodcoffee.com
℧ C

"Whether you're getting a bag of Dogwood or a cup of our coffee, know that our work is to see and give value to everyone along the way - from the people who grow our coffee to the truck driver…."

Duluth Coffee Co.
Est. 2012 by Eric Faust
105 East Superior Street
Duluth, MN 55802
Tel: 218-221-6643
duluthcoffeecompany.com
℧ S

"Eric's love for coffee connected him to wonderful people across the world. He focuses on roasting single origin coffees to pay homage to the origin and processing of coffee."

Spyhouse
Est. 2000 by Christian Johnson
2451 Nicollet Ave S.
Minneapolis, MN 55404
Tel: 612-871-3177
www.spyhousecoffee.com
FT 🌿

"We are a Twin Cities roaster and retailer that cultivates relationships with those who share our passion and vision to source, roast, and serve exceptional coffees."

Missouri

Blueprint Coffee
Est. 2013 by Andrew Timko, Brian Levine, Mike Marquard
6225 Delmar Boulevard
St. Louis, MO 63130
Tel: 314-266-6808
www.blueprintcoffee.com
☕ ℧ S C

"Roasting becomes our method to highlight…the farmer's work by finding the right balance of flavors. We define a good roast as one that showcases the best qualities of a coffee while still leaving room for interpretation."

"I judge the restaurant by the bread and by the coffee." – actor Burt Lancaster

GRAHAME'S COFFEE GUIDE

Messenger Coffee
Est. 2013 by Chris and Matt Matsch
1624 Grand Blvd.
Kansas City, MO 64108
Tel: 877-334-7660
www.messengercoffee.co

"Using our senses and two manual San Franciscan drum roasters, we are able to have complete control over the roast. The goal is to find the perfect …caramelization to balance the sweetness and complexity."

Montana

Montana Coffee Traders
Est. 1981 by R.C. Beall
5819 Hwy 93 South
Whitefish, MT 59937
Tel: 406-862-7633
www.coffeetraders.com

"We source and roast with the aim of representing the most exquisite coffee beans at their peak of flavor development…. We support sustainable practices by offering certified organic and fair trade coffees."

New Hampshire

Flight Coffee
Est.2012 by Claudia Barrett
30 Harvey Rd
Bedford, NH 03110
Tel: 603-836-6228
www.flightcoffeeco.com

"Beginning with its coffee growing partners around the world…and ending at its roasting lab and tasting room…Flight sees its coffee's story through with every cup. Transparency is the goal."

Wayfarer Roasters
Est.1981 by Karen & Reuben Bassett, Ben Bullerwell
626 Main Street
Laconia, NH 03246
Tel: 603-527-8313
www.wayfarerroasters.com

"[We] carefully oversees the roasting process to ensure all of the flavors and sweetness in each variety are highlighted. We source quality, unique and ethically derived coffee beans from all over the world."

New Jersey

Modcup
Est. 2013 by Travas Clifton
and Justin Hicks
25 Senate Place
Jersey City, NY 07306
Tel: 201-798-1666
www.modcup.com

"Coffee is one of the most complex fruits…it has the potential to display double the flavor complexity of wine. Modcup refuses to go the dark side - over roasting kills complexity and natural flavor."

Rojo's Roastery
Est. 2006 by David Waldman
243 North Union Street
Lambertville, NJ 08530
Tel: 609-397-0040
www.rojosroastery.com

"We subject green, un-roasted coffee to an in-depth series of tests measuring bean quality, consistency and potential. Then we meticulously roast and cup every sample that shows promise."

New Mexico

Michael Thomas
Est. 2004 by Michael Thomas
2900-2998 Hannett Ave NE
Albuquerque, NM, 87106
Tel: 505-504-7078
michaelthomascoffee.com

"When we import a new coffee, we create a roasting profile… After the roast has developed, we start to pulling samples every 30 seconds. The following day, we cup the samples to identify the optimal roast."

New York

Café Grumpy
Est. 2005 by Caroline Bell
199 Diamond St
Brooklyn NY 11222
718-383-0748
www.cafegrumpy.com

"We select green beans from socially and environmentally responsible producers… then spend time developing roast profiles to bring out the dynamic nuances in the beans. After roasting, we cup each batch to assure…quality."

"Women Drinking Coffee"" by Leonard Defrancei (1763)

Death Wish Coffee
Est. 2012 by Mike Brown
100 Saratoga Village Blvd,
Ballston Spa, NY 12020
Tel: 518-400-1050
www.deathwishcoffee.com
C

"Our carefully selected, perfectly roasted coffee beans produce a bold, highly caffeinated coffee blend. We strive for the best tasting and highest quality organic and fair trade beans in every bag."

Gimme! Coffee
Est. 2000 by Kevin Cuddeback
3201 Krums Corners Rd.
Ithaca, NY 14850
Tel: 877-446-6325
www.gimmecoffee.com
☕ Ⓓ Ⅾ S ✔ FT

"Gimme! Coffee has been a leader in the evolution of the third wave….keeping our eyes on the horizon. Our mission is to find beautiful coffee, to reveal it in the roast and prove it in the cup."

Joe Coffee
Est.2003 by Jonathan Rubinstein
131 West 21st Street
New York, NY 10011
Tel: 212-924-7400
www.joecoffeecompany.com
☕ Ⅾ S C

"We tend to roast our coffee on the lighter side—just enough to highlight the unique flavor profiles inherent in the coffees, which our Director of Sourcing meticulously chooses at origin."

Oslo Coffee
Est. 2003 by J.D./Kathy Merget
133 Roebling St
Brooklyn, NY 11211
Tel: 718-782-0332
www.oslocoffee.com

"Our premium coffee beans come from farmers who use ecologically and socially sustainable practices, helping to support a healthy ecosystem and to provide a fair living for their workers."

Partners Coffee
Est. 2012 by Amber Jacobsen and Adam Boyd
125 North 6th Street
Brooklyn, NY 11249
Tel: 347-457-6160
www.partnerscoffee.com

"Our story began in 2012 with an unwavering commitment to sourcing and roasting quality coffee….We source coffee from all over the world from people we know and trust…. We roast all of our coffee to order."

Sey Coffee
Est. 2011 by Tobin Polk and Lance Shnorenberg
18 Grattan St
Brooklyn, NY 11206
Tel: 347-871-1611
www.seycoffee.com

"We consider roasting to be a delicate procedure….we aim to deliver a crystal-clear expression of the inherent characteristics of each coffee at its absolute maximum potential….nothing short of beautiful."

North Carolina

Counter Culture
Est. 1995 by Brett Smith and Fred Houk
812 Mallard Avenue
Durham, NC 27701
Tel: 888-238-5282
counterculturecoffee.com

*"All coffee is roasted to order and…roasted and shipped on the next business day
We stand by the quality of every single batch we roast….Our overarching goal is to bring you the best coffee experiences possible."*

Ohio

Crimson Cup
Est. 1991 by Greg Ubert
700 Alum Creek Drive
Columbus, Ohio 43205
Tel: 614-252-3335
www.crimsoncup.com

"Sustainably sourced Crimson Cup coffee is available through a network of more than 350 independent coffee houses, grocers, college and universities, restaurants and food service operations….".

Top Shelf Coffee
Est. 1994 by Jordan Filippidis
361 Griswold St. N.E.
Warren, Ohio 44483
Tel: 330-373-1881
www.topshelfcoffee.com

"We started…with nothing but an old roaster, small grinder, leaky roof and a wallet full of dreams. What we had that wasn't old or small was our coffee….we roasted only the best obtainable Arabica beans."

Oklahoma

Elemental Coffee
Est.2008 by Laura Massenat
815 N Hudson Ave,
Oklahoma City, OK 73102
Tel: 405-663-1703
www.elementalcoffee.com

"Coffee is an agricultural product…much like a fruit or a vegetable….As our goal is to deliver coffee in its purest form…we will never try to enhance or alter its natural existence."

Topeca Coffee
Est.2005 by John Gaberino
507 S. Boston Ave.
Tulsa, OK 74103
Tel: 918-592-9090
www.topecacoffee.com

"Our family grows the coffee in El Salvador where we can oversee every step of the process….from planting the coffee plant to hand picking the ripest cherries to roasting it here in Tulsa and serving it in our own shops."

"Coffee is the gasoline of life."
– unknown

Oregon

Dutch Brothers
Est. 1994 by Dane and Travis Boersma
251 NE Agness Ave.
Grants Pass, OR 97526
Tel: 541-955-4700
www.dutchbros.com

"After three generations in the dairy business, government regulations pressed the family to sell the cows…the bros bought a double-head espresso machine...started passing out samples…and knew they had something special."

Heart Roasters
Est. 1999 by Rebekah and Wille Yli-Luoma
2111 E Burnside St.
Portland, OR 97214
Tel: 503-206-6602
www.heartroasters.com

"We secure green coffee during its peak time of the year….We believe the coffee's vibrancy is most apparent when it is fresh…. Heart travels to origin… quality control and select the best crops."

Pennsylvania

Ellis Coffee
Est. 1854 by Allen Cuthbert
2835 Bridge Street
Philadelphia, PA 19137
Tel: 800-822-3984
www.elliscoffee.com

"Our coffees are imported and roasted to provide a truly American cup….For over 150 years, these coffees have been known for great taste and enjoyed by illustrious patrons, including our nation's presidents."

La Colombe
Est. 1994 by Todd Carmichael and JP Iberti
130 South 19th Street
Philadelphia, PA 19103
Tel: 800-563-0860
www.lacolombe.com

"By sourcing and roasting with care, and borrowing on ancient and modern coffee traditions from around the world, the two have built a successful company and elevated coffee…."

ReAnimator

Est. 2011 by Mark Corpus and Mark Capriotti
4705 Pine Street
Philadelphia, PA 19143
Tel: 215-425-5805
www.reanimatorcoffee.com
Ⅾ S

"Everything we do is in the pursuit of experience. Whether that experience is traveling and sourcing coffees at origin in places like Ethiopia and Guatemala, cupping with our broker partners, roasting and tasting unique coffees…."

"Women Drinking Coffee"" by Leonard Defrancei (1763)

South Carolina

Coastal Coffee

Est.2010 by Brad Mallett
108 East 3rd North Street
Summerville, SC 29483
Tel: 843-376-4559
coastalcoffeeroasters.com
Ⅾ Ⓓ Ⓜ S 🌿

"Our vision [is] transforming the world's highest quality… beans into the best freshly roasted coffee….We use a creative, locally roasted process to bring our passion for great coffee to life in every bag."

Little River Roasting
Est.2001 by Gervais Hollowell
460 Marion Ave.
Spartanburg, SC 29306
Tel: 864-582-7900
www.littleriverroasting.com

"Great coffee begins with quality beans and is made perfect through the roasting process. The Little River Roasting crew uses a small 25-pound drum roaster… working in small batches."

South Dakota

Pure Bean Roasters
Est.2013 by Mark Royalty and Nick Reid
201 Main Street
Rapid City, SD 57701
Tel: 605-646-2722
www.purebeanroasters.com

"The company was birthed … to show the coffee world the excellent results that can come from fine air-roasted beans. From the first batch, the craft of roasting was continually perfected and level of quality has been raised."

Tennessee

Barista Parlor
Est.2011 by Andy Mumma
519B Gallatin Avenue
Nashville, TN 37206
Tel: 615-712-9766
www.baristaparlor.com

"We seek the betterment of coffee with an emphasis on ethical sourcing and sweetness in roasting. Our brewing philosophy focuses on framing both of these qualities."

Texas

Brown Coffee Co.
Est.2005 by Aaron Blanco
812 S. Alamo Street
San Antonio, TX 78205
Tel: 210-274-0702
www.browncoffeeco.com

"To elevate the coffee experience at every turn. That's our job. Since 2005, we've been San Antonio's first and favorite destination for the very best coffee experience anywhere.

Cuvée Coffee

Est.1998 by Mike McKim
2000 E. 6th Street
Austin, TX 78702
Tel: 512-264-1479
www.cuveecoffee.com

"Our skilled team of coffee roasters combine old world roasting techniques with the newest technology as they roast six days a week. Sensory equipment provides an exacting level of quality control."

Noble Coyote

Est.2011 by Kevin and Marta Sprague
819 Exposition Ave.
Dallas, TX 75226
Tel: 214-321-4321
www.noblecoyotecoffee.com

"Coffee roasting melds both art and science. The science helps produce consistency and quality. The art emerges from each roaster's unique background and roasting philosophy."

"I have measured out my life with coffee spoons." – T.S. Eliot

---

Utah

Millcreek Coffee Roasters

Est.1992 by the Brewster family
657 South Main Street
Salt Lake City, Utah 84111
Tel: 801-595-8646
www.millcreekcoffee.com

"From the start, special care was taken to profile each bean and roast it to its fullest potential. We have an assortment of blends and single-origin varietals, and continually cup new coffees to find unique offerings."

Salt Lake Roasting

Est.1981 by John Bolton
820 E 400 South
Salt Lake City, UT 84102
Tel: 801-363-7572
www.roasting.com

"Having the world's best beans doesn't mean beans unless they are roasted correctly. That's why we roast all of our coffees daily on the premises in custom batches."

Vermont

Brio
Est.2014 by Magdalena and Nate Van Dusen
266 Pine Street
Burlington, VT 05401
Tel: 802-777-6641
www.briocoffeeworks.com

"We are in a constant pursuit of the perfect roast....Our roasts focus on accentuating each coffee's sweetness and bringing out the more nuanced flavor notes and acidity."

Vermont Coffee Co.
Est.1979 by Paul Ralston
1197 Exchange Street,
Middlebury, VT 05753
Tel: 802-398-2776
vermontcoffeecompany.com

"Over the years we've developed a unique style of slow-roasting our coffee in small batches, which caramelizes the beans and brings out the semi-sweet chocolate flavors of the coffee."

Virginia

Cervantes
Est. 2011 by Marialy and Alejandro Justiniano
1370 Progress Road
Suffolk, VA 23434
Tel: 703-455-0011
www.cervantescoffee.com

"[We are] an artisan roaster specialized in single origin coffees from Central and South America....working directly with suppliers, coffee cooperatives, and individual growers, so we know where our coffee comes from."

Mudhouse
Est.1993 by Lynelle and John Lawrence
213 W. Main St.
Charlottesville, VA 22902
Tel: 434-984-6833
www.mudhouse.com

"Roasting coffee is not alchemy. Our coffee mentor once reminded us that you cannot make gold from straw. You have to start with great green beans. So every week we cup coffees from small farms across the globe."

"Man with Top Hat Drinking Coffee""
by Vincent van Gogh (1882)

www.grahamescoffeeguide.com

Washington

Broadcast Coffee
Est.2008 by Barry Fought
1918 E. Yesler Way
Seattle, WA 98122
Tel: 206-322-0807
www.broadcastcoffee.com
ⅅ S

"Barry hails from the expansive wheat fields and eep blue skies of Idaho….After college he ended up in the family business of broadcasting. But his yearning…led him to the evergreen city of Seattle."

Caffe Vita
Est.1995 by Mike McConnell
1005 E. Pike Street
Seattle, WA 98122
Tel: 302-712-2132
www.caffevita.com
☕ ⅅ S 🌿

"We use vintage Probat and Gothot roasters, allowing full manual control over the process and giving our roasters the ability to monitor and adjust every stage of flavor development in the roasting process."

Coava Coffee
Est.2008 by Matt Higgins
1300 So. Grand Ave. (A)
Portland, OR 97214
Tel: 503-894-8134
www.coavacoffee.com
ⅅ S

"Matt dreamed of starting his own company where he could roast and prepare coffees that would be exciting for professional baristas and inviting to everyday drinkers."

Elm Coffee
Est. 2013 by Brendan Mullally
240 2nd Avenue South
Seattle, WA 98104
Tel: 206-445-7808
www.elmcoffeeroasters.com
ⅅ S

"We opened Elm because we love drinking and sharing great coffee. In partnership with incredible producers and importers, we purchase exceptional green coffee and roast it for you, our customers and wholesale partners."

Olympia
Est.2005 by Sam Schroeder
600 4th Ave. East
Olympia, WA 98501
Tel: 206-360-753-0066
www.olympiacoffee.com
ⅅ S 🌿

"From varietal selection, to day lot separation, to experimental processing we have never had a greater ability to seek out and shape the flavors we want to experience in a coffee."

GRAHAME'S COFFEE GUIDE

Victrola
Est. 2000 by Chris Sharp.
Current owner: Dan Ollis.
411 15th Ave. East
Seattle, WA 98112
Tel: 206-325-6520
www.victrolacoffee.com

"Early on, we committed ourselves to the task of sourcing, roasting, and preparing the finest coffees available. Since then, innovation has marked our roasting operations and coffee preparation."

London Coffee House, 17th Century

Wisconsin

JBC Coffee Roasters
Est.1994 by Michael Johnson
5821 Femrite Drive
Madison, WI 53718
Te: 608-256-5282
www.jbccoffeeroasters.com

"Often times a producer's story lost in the coffee supply chain. It's our focus to provide a seed to cup experience, honoring everyone involved."

Ruby Coffee Roasters
Est.2013 Jared Lindsmeier
9515 Water St, Amherst Junction, WI 54407
Tel: 715-254-1592
www.rubycoffeeroasters.com

"Each of our coffees is carefully and specifically chosen to represent a glimpse of microclimate, micro-region....We focus on celebrating the unique, qualities of each offering."

Wonderstate Coffee
Est.2005 by Caleb Nicholes and TJ Semanchin
1201 N. Main Street
Viroqua, WI 54665
Tel: 608-637-2022
www.kickapoocoffee.com

"Our intimate knowledge of each harvest, and our highly tuned palates, guide us in unleashing the latent potential of each harvest. We roast in small batches to order, creating a dynamic palette of flavors."

Wyoming

Pine Coffee Supply
Est.2007 by Jim Hamilton and Tom Billonis
47 W. Pine Street
Pinedale, WY 82941
Tel: 307-367-4343
www.pinecoffeesupply.com
S

"We dedicate our passion to coffee and carefully selecting only high quality offerings….We roast to bring out and highlight the unique characteristics inherent to each coffee."

LATIN AMERICA

ARGENTINA

Café Martinez
Est.1933 by the Martinez Family
Av. Asamblea 802
C1424 Buenos Aires
Tel: +54 11 4925-8882
www.cafemartinez.com

"Through our exclusive roasting process, we highlight the notes and…of the different coffee beans. A full aroma with notes of chocolate, toasted bread, honey and caramel and a flavor with body."

Coffee Town
Est.2012 by José Vales
Bolívar 976, C1066 AAI, Buenos Aires
Tel: +54 11 4361-0019
coffeetowncompany.com
D S

"After years of touring coffee plantations, working directly with coffee growers in Latin America and Africa … we decided to create Coffee Town…with our own philosophy; offer the best coffees…at a fair price."

Delirante
Est. 2015 by José Sojo
Mitre 585
San Carlos de Bariloche
Tel: +54 9 2944 14 0550
www.cafedelirante.com.ar
S

"We are certified as a "Professional Roaster" by the Specialty Coffee Assn. and we constantly travel to continue training ourselves to produce higher quality coffee."

Lattente
Est. 2011 by Daniel Cifuentes
Thames 1891
C1414 Buenos Aires
Tel: +54 11 4833-1676
www.cafelattente.com
S C

"Coffee ain't no joke for us here at Lattente. It's our life! From flat whites to training courses, we're committed to serving up the best café in Buenos Aires."

BAHAMAS

Bahamas Coffee Roasters
Est.2013 by Kirk and Patti Aulin
Dunmore Town
Tel: 242-470-8015
www.bahamascoffee
 roasters.com
S 🌿 Ⓓ Ⓜ

"We have over 30 years' experience with coffee…. We take the green beans and slow-roast to perfection in small batches. Each batch can be blended to create a mélange of tastes unique to these Islands or remain alone from the origin grown."

"Coffee is a lot more than just a drink….It gives you time…a chance to be, like be yourself, and have a second cup."
— *Gertrude Stein*

BARBADOS

Wyndhams
Est.2001 by Dominic and Many Wyndham-Gittens
RF Humphrey Complex
Dayrells Road
Christ Church, BB14030
Tel: 246-538-1000
www.wyndhams.bb
Ⓓ S 🌿

"As family-owned coffee roasters, we are inspired by coffee at its source. The farms, the plant, the production, and the people behind the whole journey from farm to cup."

BELIZE

Caye Coffee Roasting
Est.2013 by Paul Duville
Sailfish Street, San Pedro
Tel: 502-653-4806
www.cayecoffee.bz

"We roast our coffee in small batches to capture the best flavour possible. We only use high elevation Arabica beans from Guatemala which provides us with a very full-bodied coffee product."

BERMUDA

Devil's Isle Coffee
Est.2013 by Holger Eiselt
19 Burnaby Street
Hamilton HM11
Tel: 441 292 3284
www.devilsislecoffee.bm

"We pride ourselves on the superior quality of our specialty coffee beans. Our award-winning roaster… expertly blends the beans right here in Bermuda using a 'small batch' process. This brings out unique flavor…."

Rock Island Coffee
Est.1995 by Susannah Frith and Mark Kaufman
Current owner: LIsabet Outerbridge
48 Reid Street
Hamilton HM11
Tel: 441 296 5241
www.rockisland.bm

"We source our beans from all over the world. All of our beans are roasted downstairs in the roast shack. Reid Street is frequently perfumed with our fragrant, toasted Arabica. Rock Island's walls are always decorated with fresh and interesting artwork."

BOLIVIA

Elevate Coffee
Est.2018 by Veruschka and Cliff Stevens
1143 Avenida Pando
Cochabamba
Tel: +591 76476604
www.elevate.coffee

"Our mission is to not only introduce the very best of Bolivian coffee to Bolivians… but also elevate the local coffee culture, create pride in their own amazing coffee and the producers behind it."

Valverde
Est.2004 by Nelson and Jorge Valverde
Diaz Villamil 5601
La Paz
Tel: 591-2-275-0852
www.cafevalverde.com

"Bolivia has excellent regions for growing coffee because it is both tropical…and also has very high altitudes. The higher the altitude, the longer the coffee bean takes to ripen and develop and the more pronounced its flavors will be."

"The Dining Room"" by Paul Signac (1887)

BRAZIL

Brazil is truly the behemoth of the coffee trade, exporting 5.7 billion pounds each year. That is one-third of all global exports of coffee. In fact, Brazil has been the world's largest exporter of coffee for more than 150 years – and at one time it actually supplied around 80 percent of the world's coffee. Interestingly, Brazilians only drink half as much coffee as the Finnish, who are the top global drinkers. But that still ranks the Brazilians in the Top Ten.

Academia do Café
Est. 2011 by Bruno and Debora Souza
R. Grão Pará, 1024 - Funcionários, Belo Horizonte MG, 30150-341
Tel: +55 31 3223 8565
academiadocafe.com.br

"Bruno Souza is the fourth generation of a coffee producing family…. Our coffees go through a rigorous selection process where our team score and select the best coffees…to be served in our cafeteria."

Isso é Café
Est. 1890 by Felipe Croce
R. Barão de Tatuí 183-195
Santa Cecilia, São Paulo - SP, 01226-030
Tel: +55 11 2691 5363

"This cafe was born from the desire to present everything we learned from the farm to the studio in a didactic, clear and friendly way…. We propose an invitation to change conventions."

Octavio Cafe
Est. 1890 by Giuseppe and Vicente Quercia
Rua Júlio Conceição, 553
Bom Retiro, Sao Paolo
Tel: +55 19 3795-8549
www.octaviocafe.com.br

"Producing special beans to form the unique blend of Octavio Café was not enough. It was necessary to …share all our…knowledge of coffee. Thus Octavio was born! A complete university on coffee."

Sofa Cafe
Est.2011 by Diego Gonzales
R. Bianchi Bertoldi 130 –
Pinheiros, São Paulo - SP
Tel: +55 11 3034 5830
www.sofacafe.com.br
S

"Roasting requires a lot of technical knowledge and that is why we insist on toasting all the coffee we use…to conserve the natural sugars of the grains and control other characteristics…."

Um Coffee Co.
Est.2016 by Boram Julio Um
Rua Júlio Conceição, 553
Bom Retiro, Sao Paolo
Tel: +55 11 3229-3988
www.umcoffeeco.com.br
S

"Each coffee has unique characteristics, and roasting is the moment when these unique qualities can be potentiated. That's why we created our own roasting lab."

*"Portrait of the Artist's Mother"
by Henri Toulouse-Lautrec (1881)*

www.grahamescoffeeguide.com

BRITISH VIRGIN ISLANDS

Caribbean Mountain Coffee
Est.2008 by Libbie Oliver
9718 Estate Thomas St.
Tel: 284-441-8563
www.caribbeanmountaincoffee.com

"Caribbean Mountain Coffee connects people to the Caribbean through our premium Organic coffee….we are passionate about making a difference in the lives of the families who grow and harvest the coffee."

CHILE

Café Cultura
Est.2012 by Juan Mario Carvajal
Suecia 0130, Providencia
Región Metropolitana
Tel: +56 2 2833 3183
www.cafecultura.cl

"Our mission: covering the world of high quality specialty coffee, from seed to cup….Our quality team travels to the origin of the coffee in search of the most special flavors."

"The powers of a man's mind are directly proportioned to the quantity of coffee he has drunk."

— *Sir James MacKintosh*

COLOMBIA

Spanish priests first brought coffee to Colombia in the early 1700s. It was soon adopted by local farmers and today there are some 600,000 local coffee farms, helping to make Colombia the third-largest coffee exporter in the world. The nutrient-rich soil, high elevation, and wet climate produce a flavorful coffee!

Azahar
Est.2010 by Keith Schuman and Tyler Youngblood
Av. Centenario Cra. 6
Armenia / Quindi
Tel: +57 315 371 5465
www.azaharcoffee.com

"We source our coffee from farmers all across the country and ship it around the world. But with a roastery in Quindío and a couple cafés in Bogotá ...because Colombia deserves to drink its best coffee."

Café Velvet
Est.2014 by Ilse Geyskens
Carrera 37#8a-46
Medellin
Tel: +57 4366 3788
www.cafevelvet.co

"We are highly passionate about what we do... believed the variety and complexity of tastes and aromas in Colombian coffees is immense and only at the beginning of its potential."

Hija Mia
Est.2015 by Shaun Murdoch
Calle 11a No 43b -9
Medellín, Antioquia
Tel: +57 4366 3788
www.hijamiacoffee.com

"Being a small batch roaster in Colombia ... we have the luxury of intercepting small micro lots before they get exported to bring you the very best that this wonderful country has to offer."

Juan Valdez
Est. 2002 by National Fed. of Coffee Growers
Calle 73 8 13 Bogota
Comuna Chapinero, Bogotá
Tel: +57 313 6600
www.juanvaldezcafe.com

"Our stores give you the opportunity to experience the unique flavors and aromas of 100% Colombian coffee, including an appealing portfolio of single origin coffees."

Pergamino Cafe
Est.2012 by Pedro Echaverria
Cra. 37 #8A-37
Medellín, Antioquia
Tel: +57 318 821 1303
www.us.pergamino.co
☕ S

"Great coffee has to be freshly roasted, period….You order, we roast, and you get your coffee through FedEx a couple of days later. It's simple. We do this directly from Medellin."

"Coffee" by Henri Matisse (1916)

COSTA RICA

Café Britt
Est1985 by Steve Aronson
Jaco Walk Provincia de
Puntar. Garabito 61101
Tel: 800-462-7488
www.cafebritt.com

"Café Britt not only roasts the best coffee from Costa Rica, but also from Perú, Ecuador, Mexico, Brazil, and Colombia…. we are dedicated to continuously improve and innovate."

Café Milagro
Est.1994 by Adrienne Pellizzari and Lance Byron
Av Central de Quepos
Prov. de Punt. Quepos
Tel: 506-2777-1707
www.cafebritt.com

"Cafe Milagro remains an independently owned and operated business and active member of the community. Based in Costa Rica, we are your direct source for premium, single origin, estate grown, micro milled coffees."

DOMINICAN REPUBLIC

Café Maguana
Est.2011 by Jairon Francisco
Calle Santiago No. 369,
Gazcue, Santo Domingo
Tel: 829 680 8440
www.cafemaguana.com
S

"The richness of Dominican coffee is its diversity. Depending where the coffee comes from, its flavor and aroma can be very different …we are constantly searching for new places and experiences."

ECUADOR

Fancor
Est.1985 by Steve Aronson
Av. 6 de Diciembre N31-89 Quito 170518
Tel: +593 98 025 5582
www.fancorcoffee.com

"Fancor is a sensory experience, which is perceived in each of the products we create We work with light roasts, as we consider it the best way to highlight the qualities of each coffee bean."

EL SALVADOR

Viva Espresso
Est.2005 by Frederico Bolanos
Bulevar Del Hipodromo 644
San Salvador
Tel: +503 2264 2463
www.vivaespressocoffee.com

"Coffee is our passion, … Our work starts from the selection of the best beans in farms with unique microclimates and ends with the preparation of authentic and unique drinks."

GRENADA

Spice Isle Coffee
Est.2012 by Gerald Rothaus
Frequente Industrial Park
Bldg 8, St. George's
Tel: 473-232-3000
www.grenadacoffee.com

"We import the finest quality coffee beans from all over the world - Colombia, Brazil, Ethiopia, Papua New Guinea, Uganda, Peru, Guatemala, Java, and more…. Roasting with love means getting the very best flavor from each coffee."

GUATEMALA

Godoys Gourmet
Est.195 by Steve
7a Avenida 15-85, Zona 13, Guatemala City
Tel: 502 2219-5364
www.godoyscoffee.com

"We grow, process, roast, and expoert high-quality coffee worldwide. Our farm is located in the south east corner of Guatemala … on a small volcano called Moyuta."

"Still Life with Coffee Pot" by Roger Fry (1915)

www.grahamescoffeeguide.com

JAMAICA

It was in 1728 that Sir Nicholas Lawes, Governor of Jamaica imported coffee plants into the island from Martinique, planting them in St Andrew parish. Soon enough, the industry took off. While there have been challenges over the years, Jamaican coffee is still widely considered among the best in the world, thanks to the cool, misty climate of the Blue Mountains where some of its finest beans grow. Representing just 0.1% of worldwide production today, Jamaican coffee is considered a prized possession!

Coffee Roasters
Est. 1994 by John and Mark Fletcher
69-75 Constant Spring Rd.
Kingston
Tel: 876-632-6358
www.countrytraders.com
S

"We roast our coffee in small gas-fired roasters (a Probat and a Lilla) carefully supervised by our devoted workers. As a result, we offer a subtle and multi-layered taste to our coffee."

Jablum
Est. 1923
Mavis Bank Coffee Factory
St. Andrew, Jamaica
Tel: 877-522-9603
www.jablumcoffee.com
℃ S

"Flavored by ideal altitude, mineral-rich soil, gentle cloud cover, mountain shade and ample sunlight, the berry grown in the Blue Mountains takes longer than others to mature."

Trumpet Tree
Est. 2014 by Arthur Mcgowan
Constitution Hill
St. Andrew
Tel: 647-247-0450
www.trumpettreecoffee.com
S

"Nestled at the ridge that joins Dallas Mountain with Darby peak on the world renowned Jamaica Blue Mountain – approximately 4000 ft above sea level, our highest quanlity arabica beans are grown."

Wallenford

Est. 1746 by Matthew Wallen
80 Marcus Garvey Drive
Kingston
Tel: 876-923-5850
www.wallenford.com
S

"At elevations higher than 2,000 feet above sea level, the rich soil and continuous rainfall combine to create conditions perfect for cultivating the world's most distinguished brew… famous for its rarity."

MEXICO

Coffee arrived to Mexico in the late 1700s, a bit later than other Latin American countries, but it has become one of its major crops, grown mostly in the southern states of Chiapas and Oaxaca. Today, Mexico is the world's largest producer of organic coffee. Mexican coffee beans are known to be very flavorful, boasting chocolatey and nutty qualities. Enjoy!

Blend Station

Est. 20?? by Abril Solis and Alejandro Forte
Avenida Tamaulipas 60
Col. Condesa, Hipódromo
Tel: 52 55 5086 6590
www.blendstation.com.mx

"Blend Station's specialties do justice to the principles that Alejandro set out to uphold from the beginning: a place offering a full and intelligent coffee experience …marked by equity, respect and fair trade."

Café Passmar

Est. 1995 by Salvador Benitez
Calle Adolfo Prieto s/n, Del Valle, Benito Juárez
Tel: 52 55 5669 1994
www.cafepassmar.com

"Café Passmar is a family dream in which we seek to carry out with love and passion all the processes necessary to achieve the best cups of coffee."

Chiquitito Cafe
Est. 2011 by Jeremy Clouser
Alfonso Reyes 232,
Hipódromo, Cuauhtémoc,
06100 Ciudad de México
Tel: +52 55 5211 6123
chiquititocafetienda.com

"We were born from the desire to create a community, based on fair and sustainable trade, taking care of every detail, from the producer and the grain to the barista and the cup."

NICARAGUA

Café Bristol
Est. 2008
PO Box 451404
Miami, FL 33245
Tel: 305 833-9459
www.bristolnicaragua.com
Ⓓ Ⓜ Ⓛ S

"Bristol Coffee is simply pure Arabica coffee beans, which undergo their whole production process in one place - Santa Francisca Romana Estates, located in the shaded hills of San Marcos."

"Women Drinking Coffee" by Jean-Baptish Vanmour (1700s)

PERU

Café Bisetti
Est. 1958 by Romulo Bisetti
Av. Pedro de Osma 116
Barranco, Lima
T: 01 713 9565
www.cafebisetti.com

"Bisetti was born with the aim of offering ... a sample of the best Peruvian coffee beans, which are rigorously selected, evaluated and roasted daily by our team of professional tasters, roasters and baristas."

Cate Tasting Room
Est. 2015
Calle Independencia 269
Miraflores, Lima
Tel: 01 446 3041
www.cateperu.com
Ⓓ Ⓜ Ⓛ S 🌿

"We seek to make Peruvian coffee known in all its versatility and quality to the world. We receive the beans that were grown… throughout the country and we select the best ones for each type of roasting."

TRINIDAD AND TOBAGO

Full Bloom Coffee
Est. 2018 by Kiel Robertson
2 De Verteuil Street
Port of Spain
Tel: 868-368-7159
www.fullbloomcoffeett.com
Ⓓ Ⓜ

"Our 100% premium arabica coffee beans are always sourced from ethical and environmentally responsible cooperatives. We roast in small batches every week ensuring the highest levels of freshness and flavour."

U.S. VIRGIN ISLANDS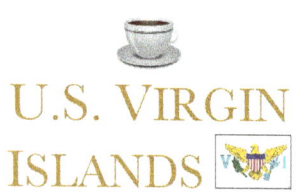

Virgin Island Coffee Roasters
Est.2012 by Ramsey Smith
9718 Estate Thomas
St. Thomas 00802
Tel: 340-201-1235
www.virginislandcoffee
 roasters.com

"The secret lies in our method of artisanal small batch roasting. Roasting our beans in smaller quantities leads to better quality control, and lets us capture flavors and aromas."

Asia, Mideast, & Africa

AUSTRALIA

Australia's great love affair with coffee is fierce and longstanding – in fact, going back to 1788 when a British fleet left England and picked up some coffee plants in Rio de Janeiro along the way. While it proved not to grow so well, Italians immigrants arriving in the 1930s brought with them their roasting knowledge and skill. Today, Australian coffee roasters are at the leading edge, producing some of the best brews anywhere.

Leftfield Coffee
Est.2014 by Louise Gordon and Kamran Nowduschani
30 Drake Street
Osborne Park, WA, 6017
Tel: +61 4 1883 2490
www.leftfieldcoffee.com
S DC M L

"Our roasters require attention to every detail which…allows us to be more connected to the roasting process to coax out the most desirable flavours for our blends and single origins coffees."

Dukes
Est.2008 by Peter Frangoulis
247 Flinders Lane
Melbourne VIC 3000
Tel: +61 3 9417 5578
www.dukescoffee.com.au

"[Our] focus is the craft of carefully roasting the best coffees in the world using innovative and methodic roasting practices. We are committed to bringing the best selection of exceptionally grown…coffees."

Industry Beans
Est. 2010 by Steve and Trevor Simmons
3/62 Rose Street
Fitzroy VIC 3065
Tel: +61 3 9417 1034
www.industrybeans.com

"Coffee [is] a natural product with many possibilities… different varietals, growing conditions, processing methods and brewing techniques could each yield something distinctive."

Single O

Est. 2003 by Dion and Emma Cohen
60-64 Reservoir Street
Surry Hills NSW 2010
Tel: +61 2 9693 2232
www.singleo.com.au
℃ S

"We are forever sourcing, sampling, cupping, roasting, measuring, calibrating, tweaking, blending & tasting….We try to source ethically & environmentally sound beans."

CHINA

Mainland

Café de Volcan

Est.2011 by Lindsay Messenger, Nils Weisensee
80 Yong Kang Road
Xuhui District, Shanghai
Tel: 86 15 61 866 9291
www.cafevolcan.com
S

"We're offering premium coffees from all over the world, including our signature beans from an award-winning coffee estate in Guatemala that has been in the family for more than 120 years."

Seesaw

Est.2012 by Tom Zong
No. 8 433 Yuyuan Road
Jingan, Shanghai
Tel: 86 21 621 46809
www.seesawcoffee.com

"There are no shortcuts to making great coffee. It involves many sleepless nights and commitment…. We are where we are today in no small part to the 25 Yunnan farmers we have worked with."

"A cup of coffee shared with a friend is happiness tasted and time well spent."
— *Unknown*

Hong Kong

Hazel & Hershey
Est.2012 by Birdie Chiu
Shop 3, 69 Peel St,
Hong Kong Central
Tel: +852 3106 0760
www.hazelnhershey.com

"At Chung Wo Lane…we started our first coffee roastery, locally turning raw coffee beans imported from different parts of the world into ready grind and brew coffee beans."

Urban Coffee Roaster
Est.2014 by Gary Au and Horry Cheung
7 Bristol Avenue
Tsim Sha Tsui
Tel: 852 2363 3661
www.ucr.hk

"Quality and consistency have always been our first priority. To accomplish this, we have a modern plant with cutting edge facilities together with a team comprised of sourcing, roasting, quality control, sensory, brewing expertise.

*"Vase with Flowers, Coffeepot, and Fruit"
by Vincent Van Gogh, 1887*

www.grahamescoffeeguide.com

ETHIOPIA

Coffee's origins trace back to Ethiopia. According to legend, coffee was discovered by a goat herder named Kaldi, who found that his flock was bursting with energy after eating the red fruit of a coffee shrub. Kaldi tried the fruit for himself and had a similar reaction, so he brought the berries to a nearby monastery where the monks did some experimenting. Lo and behold, they produced coffee! Today, Ethiopia still produces coffee beans along with some fine roasters such as those below:

Fili Coffee
Est.2016 by Filimon T/Selassie
Lafto around 2000 Bldg.
Addis Ababa
Tel: +251 911 029 370
www.filicoffee.com
S

"Our philosophy is driven by a passion for coffee and commitment to source and roast some of the highest quality Ethiopian coffee… from different regions of Ethiopia."

Garden of Coffee
Est.2014 by Bethlehem Tilahun Alemu
Adams Pavillioin, 4th Flr.
Addis Ababa
Tel: 251-911 110 848
www.gardenofcoffee.com
S

"In Ethiopia we don't just grow coffee….It's embedded in the DNA of our daily life. Coffee personifies Ethiopia and we personify it…I began Garden of Coffee so that people everywhere can experience that magic."

Tomoca Coffee
Est.1953 by Wondwossen Meshesha
Wawel Street
Addis Ababa
Tel: +251 93 007 8086
www.tomocacoffee.com
S

"Here in Tomoca, we share and converse with friends around coffee, showing love and respect…as this tradition has been kept for years. We are keen towards having an Ethiopian taste alongside all its traditional values."

INDIA

It is said that in the 1500s a sufi named Baba Budan brought some coffee beans back with him from a pilgrimage to Mecca. Initially, India grew Arabica beans but after an infestation switched to Robusta. It's worked well. India is today the world's 7th largest coffee producer.

Araku Coffee
Est. 2001 by Manoj Kumar
502, Trendset Towers,
Road No.2 Banjara Hills,
Hyderabad
www.arakucoffee.in
S

"Araku has been created by the coming together of international coffee experts and the farmers of our cooperative. Together, they have [creaed] the first fully integrated value chain of coffee."

"Enjoying Coffee" (Turkey, early 18th century)

Blue Tokai
Est. 2013 by Namrata Asthana and Matt Chitharanjan
33 New Kant Wadi Lane,
Bandra West, Mumbai,
Maharashtra 400050
Tel: +91 90825 66400
www.bluetokaicoffee.com

"We are consistently researching best practices …making refractometers essential for our cafe brewing, holding advanced sensory learnings for junior roasters, and experimenting with processing at the farm level."

Flying Squirrel
Est. 2013 by Ashish D'Abreo and Tej Thammaiah
Ground Flr #1, Teachers Colony, Bangalore-560043
Tel: +91 9845153587
www.flyingsquirrel.in

"We grow our coffee in the midst of citrus patches, vanilla plantations, spice patches…so the finer nuances and characteristics of our final coffee have a wide canvas to develop from."

KC Roasters
Est. 2017 by Shannon D'Souza and Clement Sissia
6, Chuim Village Rd, Khar, Khar West, Mumbai
Tel: +91 91366 50277
www.kcroasters.com
℃ S Ⓓ Ⓜ C

"Each batch of our hand-selected coffee is sampled before being roasted in our top-of-the-line Probat Roaster…. We take the beans on a journey as we attempt to either highlight or layer its inherent flavours."

INDONESIA

Anomali Coffee
Est. 2007 by Irvan Helmi
Iskandarsyah Raya No.19
Jakarta 12190
Tel: +62 21 52920102
www.anomalicoffee.com
S

"Anomali Coffee presents various flavors of Indonesian specialty coffee with unique authentic taste and aroma. The products are made passionately using only the best quality ingredients."

Common Grounds
Est. 2010 Aston Utan, Yoshua Tanu, and Daryanto Witarsa
Citywalk Sudirman GF No. Kav. 121, Jakarta 10250
Tel: +62 21 25558963
www.commongrounds.co.id
☕ S

"We are obsessed about how good coffee is crafted. Whether brewed meticulously over filters, or carefully prepared as an espresso, our goal is to show you coffee's delicious possibilities."

Gerilya Coffee
Est. 2016 Gerilya Adhidrawa Prakasa
Jalan Banjarsari I No.8A, RT.1/RW.8, Jakarta 12430
Tel: +62 21 27828901
www.gerilya.id
☕ S

"Our vision: to make Gerilya Coffee and Roastery… focused on quality and be responsible for the sustainability of Indonesian coffee industry from farm to cup."

Maharaja Coffee
Est. 2009 by Kasmito T
Jl. Melawan No.26/4, RT.7/RW.7 Daerah Khusus Ibukota Jakarta 10730
Tel: +62 21 6248148
www.maharaja.coffee
S

*"We seek to show the diversity of Indonesia…. we collect coffee samples from every part of Indonesia… from farmers we have been working with for a decade…
We keep learning about the coffee, origin, sub-varieties."*

ISRAEL

Aroma
Est.1994 by Sahar Shefa
18 Hillel Street
Jerusalem 9458118
Tel: 972-2-625-5365
www.aroma.us

"Aroma's state-of-the-art roasting house roasts beans five days a week and packs them in our unique valve and vacuum-sealed packages. Our flavorful coffee beans are then continually shipped to branches worldwide."

Cafelix

Est. 2011 by Philipp and Yael Schaefer
15 Sgula Street
Tel Aviv-Yafo
Tel: 972 3-546-9890
www.cafelix.co.il
S D

"We source and import high quality coffees from motivated and knowledgeable farmers… We handcraft each batch with our special roasting equipment … We are stubborn, resist following changing trends and fashions."

Kilimanjaro Coffee

Est. 2016 by David Strausberg
Hoshaya 17915
Tel: 972 54 250 9120
www.kilimancoffee.com
☕ D S C

"I spent 6 weeks in Moshi, a smallish city in the foothills of Mt. Kilimanjaro. While there I fell in love with the coffee from the mountain, and on the flight back it I realized that I wanted to share truly great coffee like this with others"

JAPAN

Beer Pond Espresso

Est. 2009 by Katsu Tanaka
2 Chome-36-12 Kitazawa,
Setagaya, Tokyo 155-0031
Tel: +81 3 5454 2486
www.beerpondespresso roasters.com

"All of our coffee is harvested at the peak of their flavor. Our roasting techniques are designed to enhance the location, elevations, soils and climate that give each coffee a unique individuality."

Frankie

Est. 2015 by Alex Daniel
2 Chome-12-15 Kitazawa
Tokyo 155-0031
Tel: +81 3-6356-5305
www.frankie.jp
S

"Frankie offers premium quality espresso coffee from Allpress Espresso – freshly roasted…from a blend of Arabica beans sourced direct from farmers in Guatemala, Brazil, Columbia, and Sumatra."

Glitch Coffee
Est.2015 by Kiyokazu Suzuki
1F 3-16 Kanda-Nishikicho
Chiyoda-Ku,Tokyo 101-0054
Tel: +81 3 5244 5458
www.glitchcoffee.com
S

"We provide a cup of value by strictly focusing on not only roasting and brewing, but also cultivation, purification …..Our coffee expresses the character of single origin beans by super light roasting."

LEBANON

Kalei Coffee
Est.2015 by Dalia Jaffal
Next to the Inaash Association
Beirut
Tel: +961 1 752 001
www.kaleicoffee.com
S

"As coffee enthusiasts, we travel the world to see what flavors countries have to offer…. Our aim is simple: people need to see the potential of specialty coffee."

MALAYSIA

Roast Things, The
Est. 2015 by Chiam Tow Jin
A-G-01, Prima Avenue,
The Tube Jalan PJU 1/39,
Dataran Prima 47301
Tel: +60 3-5879 8392
www.theroastthings.com
S

"We do not believe in over roasting coffees. We develop our coffees well enough that it still encap-sulates the enzymatic compounds of a coffee without under-developing its core."

Yit Foh Tanem
Est.1960 by Yong Loong Vun
3 KM Jalan Tenom Sapong
Kg. Chinta Mata
Tel: +60 6 087 735 657
www.yitfohcoffee.com
S

"Besides its unique aroma, Yit Foh's coffee also has an authentically traditional flavour. This distinctiveness comes from its coffee beans which are roasted in traditional wood-fire drum."

NEW ZEALAND

Atomic Coffee
Est.1992 by Dave Thomas
420c New North Road,
Kingsland, Auckland 1021
Tel: +64 800 286 642
www.atomiccoffee.co.nz

"Every coffee has a different make-up and unique terroir, so we roast the components of our blends individually…. The result is a range of espresso blends and single origins that are complex."

Coffee Supreme
Est.1993 by Chris Dillon and Maggie Wells
35 Hopper St, Mount Cook
Wellington 6011
Tel: +64 800 472 518
www.coffeesupreme.com

"Since coffee began, it has been central to many cultures' comings-together, regardless of class or standing. It has become synonymous with generosity and sharing, and these are values we love."

Flight Coffee
Est. 2009 by Richard Corney
30 Garrett St, Te Aro
Wellington, 6011
Tel: +64 04 212 4547
www.flightcoffee.col.nz
S

"Flight Coffee is a family of driven people that work together to produce amazing coffee, while always aiming to have the best impact we can on the industry and the lives it connects.

Red Rabbit
Est.2013 by Steve Barrett
7 Faraday Street, Parnell
Auckland 1052
Tel: +64 21 161 6607
www.redrabbitcoffee.co.nz

"Crafting clean, sweet, seasonal espresso blends and filter coffees to passionately prepare for you. To share the labyrinth of flavour in the cup you drink is what excites us."

"If it weren't for coffee, I'd have no identifiable personality whatsoever."
– David Letterman

PHILIPPINES

Kalsada
Est. 2015 by Carmel Laurino
413 Escolta St, Binondo
1008 Metro Manila
Tel: +63277517435
www.kalsada.com
S

"Our top priority is to support Filipino coffee producers and their dedicated efforts to bring quality coffee to market…. Through our work, we hope to encourage future genera-tions of Filipino coffee growers."

SAO TOME

Claudio Corallo
Est. 1992 by Claudio Corallo
Av. 12 de Julho n° 978
CP 678 São Tomé
Tel: +239 222 2236
www.claudiocorallo.com

"Half way up the highest mountain on Sao Tome lies the plantation of Nova Moca. Here Claudio and his team cultivate the different varieties of Arabica on terraces protected by stone walls."

SINGAPORE

Common Man
Est. 2013 by Harry Grover
22 Martin Rd, #01-00
Singapore 239058
Tel: +65 6836 4695
www.commonmancoffee roasters.com

"We roast almost daily to order and make sure we evaluate our coffee through cuppings on a weekly basis to ensure a fresh and consistent product."

Nylon Coffee

Est.2012 by Dennis and Jia Min
4 Everton Park #01-40
Singapore 080004
Tel: +65 6220-2330
www.nyloncoffee.sg
S

"We are firm believers of working closely with… producers. We travel long distances to visit farms and cooperatives to see for ourselves the hard work put into the coffees that we are buying."

SOUTH AFRICA

Bean There

Est.2005 by Jon Robinson
44 Stanley Ave, Milpark
Johannesburg 2092
Tel: +27 87 310 3100
www.beanthere.co.za
DC S

"Our single-origin coffee beans can be traced down to one country or region….Each conveys a unique taste of place, a compelling flavor window into the singular growing conditions."

Espressolab

Est. 2009 Renato Correia and Helene Vaerlien
375 Albert Rd, Woodstock
Cape Town 7925
Tel: +27 21 447 0845
www.espressolabmicroroasters.com
 S

"We showcase coffees from fully traceable farms, estates and cooperatives and look to establish relationships with growers and exporters, always looking at sustainable, fair and equal trade."

Port of Mocha, Yemen (1680)

SOUTH KOREA

Namusairo
Est. 2002 by Jun Sun Bae
21 Sajik-ro 8-gil, Sajik-dong
Jongno-gu, Seoul
Tel: +82-070-7590-0845
www.namusairo.com

"We are constantly visiting and communicating with our coffee farmers. Our aim is to introduce the many sides and charms of coffee using good ingredients… roasting with rigorous quality control."

TAIWAN

Fika Fika Café
Est. 2013 by Chen Zhihuang
No. 33 Yitong Street
Zhongshan District, Taipei
Tel: +886 2 2507 0633
www.fikafikacafe.com

"We hope that every customer who steps into the store can enjoy the Scandinavian vision, smell and taste….We care about every customer, every drop of coffee, every coffee bean sold.

THAILAND

Brave Roasters
Est.2013 by E. Wipawasuthi, S. Chanmantana, Nirodha V.
Soi Phanit Anan Yeak 12
Klongton-Nua, Wattana
Bangkok 10110
Tel: +66-95-947-0238
www.braveroasters.com
S C

"Brave Roasters has grown from years of working with both local and global suppliers….[We] strive to break through barriers by constantly improving and seeking new tastes, flavors, and experiences."

Roots Coffee

Est.2013 by Varatt Vichit-Vadakan
126 Soi Saladaeng 1
Silom, Bangkok 10500
Tel: +66 80-958-0255
www.rootsbkk.com

"We are a small team of coffee fanatics...devoting our resources to improving the well-being of every single person involved in the journey of our coffee - from baristas, to roasters, to farmers."

Coffee House in Constantinople by Ivan Aivazosky

TURKEY

Petra Roasting
Est. 2014 by Kaan Bergsen
Gayrettepe, Hoşsohbet
Sokağı Selenium
34349 Beşiktaş/İstanbul
Tel: +90 212 356 10 57
www.petracoffee.com
S C

"Our general philosophy is to take a humble stance in front of coffee.... Our dream was to create the coffee shop that will become a classic from the first day it opened its doors and will inspire everyone."

Spada Coffee
Est. by Cumhur Kilic
Av. Süreyya Ağaoğlu Sk.
No:8/E, Teşvikiye
34365 Şişli/İstanbul
Tel: +90 536 399 99 89
www.spadacoffee.com
S

"Each bean is roasted according to the soil structure and climate conditions of the region where it is grown, and the processing methods.... We take care to present the flavors in it with all its brightness."

UNITED ARAB EMIRATES

Jebena
Est. 2016 Stuart Szabo
Dubai Investment Park 2
Dubai
Tel: +971 4 880 0022
www.jebenacoffees.com
S

"Jebena Specialty Coffee was born from a passion for coffee, a desire to source the world's finest beans, then roast to highlight the unique natural flavours that each coffee has to offer."

VIETNAM

Saigon Coffee Roastery
Est. 2016 by Phap Vo
5 Đồng Khởi, Street Quận
1 Hồ Chí Minh 70000
Tel: +84 93 880 83 85
saigoncoffeeroastery.com
S

"We use a combination of quality green beans from Dalat and around the world such as Kenya, Ethiopia, Elsalvado ...skillfully roasted with modern machinery and expertise of the barista will bring you interesting coffee!"

COFFEE FESTIVALS

For those who *really* like coffee, below are some festivals you can attend in your city or perhaps on your next vacation. Listed to the right is the month when the festival is typically held.

Global

Global Coffee Festival www.globalcoffeefestival.com	October

Austria

Vienna Coffee Festival www.viennacoffeefestival.cc	January

Brazil

Brazil International Coffee Week www.semanainternacionaldocafe.com.br	November
Sao Paulo Coffee Festival www.saopaulocoffeefestival.com.br	June

Canada

Ottawa Coffee Fest www.ottowacoffeefest.ca	March
Toronto Coffee Festival www.toronto-coffeefestival.com	October

Finland

Helsinki Coffee Festival www.helsinkicoffeefestival.com	April

France

Paris Coffee Show — September
www.pariscoffeeshow.fr

Greece

Athens Coffee Festival — September
www.athenscoffeefestival.gr

Italy

Milan Coffee Festival — September
www.milancoffeefestival.com

Turin Coffee Week — September
www.turincoffee.it

Netherlands

Amsterdam Coffee Festival — March
www.amsterdamcoffeefestival.com

South Africa

Cape Town Coffee Festival — May
www.capetown-coffeefestival.com

United Kingdom

Glasgow Coffee Festival — October
www.glasgowcoffeefestival.com

London Coffee Festival — April
www.londoncoffeefestival.com

UNITED STATES

California

L.A. Coffee Festival — February
www.la-coffeefestival.com

San Francisco Coffee Festival — November
www.sfcoffeefestival.com

Colorado

Caffeine Crawl — September
www.caffeinecrawl.com

Florida

Tampa Bay Coffee and Art Festival — October
www.tampabaycoffeeandartfestival.com

Hawaii

Kona Coffee Cultural Festival — November
www.konacoffeefest.com

New Mexico

Southwest Chocolate and Coffee Fest — March
www.chocolateandcoffeefest.com

New York

NYC Craft Coffee Fest — September
www.nyccraftcoffeefest.com

New York Coffee Festival — October
www.newyorkcoffeefestival.com

Ohio

Cincinnati Coffee Festival — September
www.cincinnaticoffeefestival.com

Pennsylvania

Coffee and Tea Festival Philly — December
www.coffeeandteafestival.com

South Carolina

Charleston Coffee Fest — February
www.charlestoncoffeefest.com

Texas

Coffee Fest San Antonio — June
www.coffeefest.com

Houston Coffee Festival — February
www.htxcoffeefestival.com

Washington

Coffee Fest PNW — October
www.coffeefestival.com/pnw

COFFEE GLOSSARY

Acidity – The pleasant, tarty taste of a coffee
American Roast – A medium roast as found in the U.S.
Americano -- A shot of Espresso with added hot water.
Arabica – Earliest and most widely grown type of coffee tree
Aroma – Fragrance released from a cup of brewed coffee
Barista – Italian term for an experienced coffee bartender
Batch Roaster – A machine which roasts a given quantity of beans at a time.
Blend – A mixture of two or more coffee varieties.
Bourbon – An heirloom variety of Arabica beans
Caffé Latte – Espresso made with more milk than a cappuccino but only a small amount of foam.
Capuccino – Espresso with foamed milk and containing equal parts espresso, steamed milk and foamed milk.
Cold-Water Method – Coffee grounds steeped in cold water for 10-20 hours, then strained and mixed with hot water.
Cupping – A technique used by tasters to sample coffee.
Dark Roast – Coffee beans roasted to a medium-dark color.
Decaffeinated – Coffee beans which have had most of the caffeine removed.
Demitasse – Small cup used for Turkish or espresso coffee.
Doppio -- a double espresso.
Drip Coffee -- Brewing method where hot water settles through a bed of ground coffee.

Espresso – Coffee made by forcing a small amount of nearly boiling water through finely-ground coffee beans.

French Roast – Coffee beans that have been roasted to a very dark brown color.

Green Coffee – Unroasted coffee beans.

Java – Indonesian coffee from the island of Java.

Kona – Coffee beans from the Kona coast of Hawaii.

Light Roast -- Coffee beans that have not been roasted long enough to produce caramelized sugars or oil.

Lungo -- An espresso made with more water.

Macchiato -- Espresso that is "marked" with a dollop of steamed milk on top.

Neapolitan Roast – Coffee beans that are roasted darker than an espresso but not quite black.

Ristretto – An espresso made with less water.

Robusta – A type of coffee bean that is smaller and more bitter than the Arabica bean, and often used for instant coffee.

Single Origin – A coffee bean from a single country, region or batch.

Supremo – The highest grade of Colombian coffee.

Typica – One of the oldest coffee varieties.

Varietal – A single botanical type of coffee tree.

Viennese Roast – The lightest type of dark roasts that is complete just after the first crack.

COFFEE, FAIR TRADE & SUSTAINABILITY

Be a happy and responsible coffee drinker!
Learn more about these organizations:

Fair Trade Certified
1500 Broadway, Ste 400
Oakland, CA 94612
Tel: 510-663-5260
www.fairtradecertified.org

Fair Trade International
Bonner Talweg 177
53129 Bonn, Germany
Tel: +49 228 949230
www.fairtrade.net

Smithsonian / Bird Friendly Coffee
3001 Connecticut Ave., NW
Washington, DC 20008
Tel: 202-633-4888
www.nationalzoo.si.edu/migratory-birds/bird-friendly-coffee

USDA Organic
1400 Independence Ave., SE
Washington, DC 20003
Tel: 202-720-2791
www.usda.gov/topics/organic

Utz / Rainforest Alliance
De Ruyterkade 6
1013 AA, Amsterdam, Netherlands
Tel: +31 20 530 8000
www.utz.org

COFFEE IN 95 LANGUAGES

Afrikaans – koffie
Albanian – kafe
Amharic - ቡና
Arabic - قهوة
Armenian – սուրճ
Azerbaijani - qəhvə
Basque – kafea
Belarusian – кава
Bengali - কফি
Bosnian – kafu
Bulgarian – кафе

Catalan – cafè
Chichewa – khofi
Chinese - 咖啡
Croatian – kava
Czech – káva

Danish – kaffe
Dutch – koffie

Esperanto – kafo
Estonian – kohv

Filipino – kape
Finnish – kahvia
French – café
Frisian – kofje

Galician – café
Georgian - ყავა
German – kaffee
Greek – καφές
Gujarati - કોફી

Haitian – kafe
Hausa – kofi
Hawaiian – kope
Hebrew – קפה
Hindi – कॉफी
Hungarian – kávé

Icelandic – kaffi
Indonesia – kopi
Irish – caife
Italian – caffè

Japanese - コーヒー
Javanese – kopi

Kannada - ಕಾಫಿ
Kazakh – кофе
Korean – 커피
Kurdish – qehwe
Kyrgyz – кофе

Lao - ກາເຟ
Latin – capulus
Latvian – kafija
Lithuanian – kavos

Macedonian – кафе
Malagasy – kafe
Malay – kopi
Malayalam - കോഫി
Maltese – kafè
Maori – kawhe
Marathi - कॉफी
Mongolian – кофе
Myanmar - ကော်ဖီ

Nepali - कफी
Norwegian – kaffe

Pashto – کافي
Persian – کافی
Polish – kawa
Portuguese – café
Punjabi - ਕਾਫੀ

Romanian – cafea
Russian – кофе

Samoan – sukalati
Scotts Gaelic – seoclaid
Serbian – чоколада
Sesotho – tsokolate
Sindhi – چاڪليٽ
Slovak – čokoláda
Slovenian – čokolada
Somali – shukulaatada
Spanish – chocolate
Sundanese – coklat
Swahili – chokoleti
Swedish – choklad

Tajik – қаҳва
Tamil - கொட்டைவடி நீர்
Telugu - కాఫీ

Thai – กาแฟ
Turkish – kahve

Ukranian – кава
Urdu – کافی
Uzbek – qahva

Vietnamese - cà phê

Welsh – coffi

Xhosa – kofu

Yiddish – קאַווע
Yoruba – kọfi

Zulu – ikhofi

www.grahamescoffeeguide.com

ALPHABETICAL INDEX

A

Academia do Café	80
Alaska Artisan Coffee	50
Alaska Coffee Roasting	50
Anomali Coffee	99
Araku	98
Ariosa Coffee	29
Aroma Coffee	100
Artisan Roast	41
Atomic Coffee	103
Azahar	83

B

Back to Black	33
Badger & Dodo	29
Bahamas Coffee	77
Barista Parlor	68
Barn, The	25
Been There	105
Beer Pond	101
Belleville	24
Big Island Coffee	54
Big Shoulders Coffee	55
Blue Bird	28
Blue Bottle	51
Blue Tokai	99
Blueprint Coffee	60
Bocca	33
Bonanza	25
Booinga	36
Brave Roasters	106
Brio	70
Broadcast Coffee	72
Brown Coffee	68

C

Café Britt	85
Café Cultura	82
Café de Vulcan	95
Café Grumpy	62
Café Maguana	85
Café Martinez	76
Café Milagro	85
Café Passmar	89
Café Velvet	83
Cafelix	101
Caffè Nerro	41
Caffe Vita	72
Caffenation	17
Caravan Coffee	41
Caribbean Mountain	82
Caye Coffee Roasters	78
Cervantes	70
Chock full o'Nuts	48
Claudio Corallo	104
Coastal Coffee	67
Coava Coffee	72
Coffee Bean&Tea Leaf	51
Coffee Beanery	58
Coffee Collective	20
Coffee by Design	57
Coffee Island	26
Coffee Proficiency	35
Coffee Supreme	103

Coffee Tow	76		**F**	
CoffeePirate	16		Fabrica	36
Cogito	18		Fancor	86
Combi	36		Fika Fika	106
Common Grounds	100		Fili Coffee	97
Common Man	104		Filicori Zecchini	31
Community Coffee	57		Five Elephant	26
Counter Culture	64		Flight Coffee	61
Coutume	24		Flying Squirrel	99
Crimson Cup	65		Folger's	48
Cuvée Coffee	69		Frankie	101
			Frolikova Kava	20
D				
Dabov	18		**G**	
De Mello Palheta	46		Gardelli	31
Death Wish Coffee	63		Garden of Coffee	97
Delirante	77		George Howell	58
Delta Cafes	36		Gerylia	100
Devil's Isle Coffee	78		Gimme! Coffee	63
Dispatch	46		Glitch Coffee	102
Ditta Artigianale	31		Good Life Coffee	22
D'Origen	38			
Dogwood Coffee	60		**H**	
Doubleshot	20		Hawaii Island Kona	55
Dr. Wakefield	42		Hazel & Hershey	96
Drop	39		Heart Roasters	66
Drupa	33		Hija Mia	83
Dublin Coffee	57		Hola Coffee	38
Dukes	94		Hoppenworth & Pl.	26
Dunn Brothers	60		Huckleberry	52
Dutch Brothers	66			
			I	
E			Industry Beans	94
El Magnifico	38		Intelligentsia Coffee	55
Elemental Coffee	65		Isso é Café	80
Elevate Coffee	79			
Ellis Coffee	66		**J**	
Elm Coffee Roasters	72		Java Blend	45
Equator Coffee	52		JBC Coffee Roasters	73
Espresso Lab	105		Jebena	108

Jittery Joe's	54	**N**	
Joe Coffee	63	Namusairo	106
Johan & Nystrom	39	Nektar	47
Jonas Reindl	16	New England Coffee	58
Juan Valdez	83	Noble Coyote	69
Julias Meinl	16	Nomad Coffee	39
		Nylon Coffee	105

K

Kalei Coffee	102	**O**	
Kalsada	104	Octavio Café	80
KC Roasters	99	Olympia Coffee	72
Kilimanjaro Coffee	101	Onyx Coffee La	51
Knopes	32	Or Coffee	18
Koa Coffee	55	Origin	42
		Oslo Coffee	64

L

La Colombe	66	**P**	
LA Mill	52	Panther Coffee	54
La Torrefazione	22	Partners Coffee	64
Lattente	77	Paulig	23
Leftfield Coffee	94	Peet's Coffee & Tea	49
Little River	68	Pergamino Café	84
Lomi	24	Peter Larsen	21
		Petra Roasting	108

M

Madcap Coffee	59	Phil & Sebastian	45
Maeskes Roem	17	Philz Coffee	52
Maharaja Coffee	100	Pilot	46
Mame	40	Pine Coffee Supply	74
Man vs. Machine	26	Ponaire	29
Maxwell House	48	Press Coffee	51
Merrild	21	Propeller	46
Messenger Coffee	61	PT's Coffee	56
Michael Thomas	62	Pure Bean Roasters	68
Milano	45		
Millcreek Coffee	69	**Q**	
Modcup	62	Quills Coffee	56
MOK Coffee	18		
Mokkamestarit	22	**R**	
Montana Coffee	61	Rauwolf	16
Mudhouse	70	Reanimator	67

www.grahamescoffeeguide.com

Red Diamond	49
Red Rabbi	103
Revelator	49
Reykjavik Roasters	28
Rich Coffee	19
Right Side	39
Rock Island Coffe	78
Roast Things, The	102
Rojo's Roastery	62
Roots Coffee	107
Ruby Coffee	73

S

Saigon Coffee	109
Salt Lake Roasting	69
Sciascia	31
Second Cup	44
Seesaw	95
Shelbourne Falls	58
Sey Coffee	64
Silverskin	29
Single O	95
Sofa Café	81
Spada	108
Spice Isle	86
Spyhouse	60
Stockfleths	34
Stumptown Coffee	49
Supreme Roastw.	34
Sweet Beans	37
Sweet Bloom	53
Swing's Coffe	53

T

Taste Map	32
Terres de Café	24
Tim Hortons	44
Tim Wendelboe	34
Timbertrain	45
Tomoca	97
Top Shelf	65
Topeca Coffee	65

U

Um Coffee Co.	81
Urban Coffee	96

V

Valmandin	40
Valverd	79
Van Houtte	44
Vergnano	30
Verlet	25
Vermont Coffee Co.	70
Verve	52
Victrola	73
Virgin Island	92
Viva Espresso	86

W

Wallenford	89
Wayfarer Roasters	61
White Label	33
Wonderstate	74
Wyndhams	77

Y

Yit For Tanem	102

www.grahamescoffeeguide.com

Is there a coffee roaster you love and would like to recommend?

*Please write to us at:
listings@
grahamesguides.com*

Interested in buying

10

or more copies?

*Just call or write us for
our discount schedule:*

*info@grahamesguides.com
Tel: 646-907-9316*